THE ELECTRIC PRESSURE
COOKER SOUP COOKBOOK

THE ELECTRIC PRESSURE COOKER SOUP COOKBOOK

100 FAST AND FLAVORFUL RECIPES

Karen Lee Young

Photography by Darren Muir

ROCKRIDGE PRESS

For general information on our other products and services or to obtain technical support, please contact our Customer Care Department within the United States at (866) 744-2665, or outside the United States at (510) 253-0500.

Rockridge Press publishes its books in a variety of electronic and print formats. Some content that appears in print may not be available in electronic books, and vice versa.

Cover Designer: Lisa Forde
Interior Designer: John Clifford
Art Producer: Janice Ackerman
Editor: Gurvinder Singh Gandu
Production Editor: Mia Moran
Photography © 2020 Darren Muir. Food styling by Yolanda Muir.

ISBN: Print 978-1-64739-659-6 | eBook 978-1-64739-660-2

R0

To our daughter:
I hope you'll someday discover
the joy of cooking and share it
with those you love.

Contents

Introduction

For many, soup means comfort. Soup takes me back to my mother's kitchen in my childhood home, where she would have a pot simmering low and slow on the stove all day, filling the house with rich, warming aromas.

Fast-forward to my college years, when I began learning to cook. Some of the first things I was able to successfully make were soups and stews. I was amazed at how easy it was to put a few ingredients into a pot and turn them into delicious meals, using simple cooking techniques without compromising on the flavors. It was definitely a confidence booster! In fact, so much of what I know about cooking now came from making many pots of soup.

From quick, simple broths to rich, hearty stews and chowders, soups please every palate year-round and are a great way to enjoy seasonal ingredients. In spring, the time is right for some light and bright soups with vegetables that are at their prime, such as peas, asparagus, and broccoli. In the summer, I love making corn chowder with freshly shucked sweet corn or tomato basil bisque with juicy, vine-ripened tomatoes. And when it comes to the fall and winter, I move on to the heartier soups and stews featuring pumpkin, sweet potatoes, and butternut squash.

Soups are the perfect one-pot meal and make for easy dinner solutions or quick lunches, but making soup is often associated with a long cooking process. Luckily, electric pressure cooking provides all the satisfaction of flavorful, slow-simmered soups in a fraction of the time. With the electric pressure cooker, gone are the days when you need to actively stir a pot for hours.

The electric pressure cooker has quickly become one of the most popular kitchen appliances for home cooks. I'll be honest—the first time I used my electric pressure cooker, I was a bit overwhelmed and intimidated by the different buttons, settings, safety instructions, and pressure release methods. But now that I'm familiar with the basics, I can't do without this versatile, user-friendly kitchen appliance. It saves me so much effort and time when creating quick, healthy meals.

The recipes in this cookbook reflect how I like to cook for my family—with fresh, wholesome, unprocessed foods. To make meal prepping a breeze, I've adapted many of my tried-and-true soup recipes to be made with an electric pressure cooker. You'll find uncomplicated electric pressure cooker recipes that allow you to turn simple pantry staples into delicious, flavorful soups, homemade stocks, and stews with minimal effort and time. This book is designed for just about anyone, whether you're new to the electric pressure cooker or just looking for different tastes to add to your rotation. From classic French Onion Soup (page 24) to Vietnamese-Inspired Beef Pho (page 160) and Smoked Sausage and Seafood Gumbo (page 182), I'm sure there's a soup recipe you'll enjoy. So, grab that electric pressure cooker and some fresh ingredients, and let's get cooking!

CHAPTER 1

MAKING SOUP IN AN INSTANT

With the electric pressure cooker, making soup is as easy as a bit of prep and pressing a button or two. In this chapter, we'll go over the basics of making soup in the electric pressure cooker, including the benefits and safety precautions. I will also highlight some of the kitchen tools that will help you along the way, as well as the essential ingredients that you'll need for making soup.

BENEFITS OF COOKING SOUP IN AN ELECTRIC PRESSURE COOKER

With its wide range of programmable settings, the electric pressure cooker is an extremely versatile kitchen appliance. While the types of dishes that you can cook with this appliance are virtually limitless, soups are among my favorite choices. There are many benefits to this method over traditional stovetop cooking. Here are some top reasons:

One-pot convenience

Unlike a slow cooker, the electric pressure cooker is a one-pot system that allows you to sauté aromatics like onions and garlic and brown meat to develop layers of flavors before cooking them under pressure. If you need to simmer and thicken your soup after pressure cooking, you can do so right in the cooker. And there's no need to use multiple pots and pans, which means less time spent cleaning.

Set it and forget it

Most of the recipes in this book call for a few minutes of prep time and zero hands-on time during the actual cooking. Since the electric pressure cooker is fully automated, once it's set, you don't have to worry about the temperature or pressure settings. There is no need to stir or watch the food as it cooks, and there is very little risk of burning food in the electric pressure cooker, which makes it a perfect fit for the busy cook.

Save time

Electric pressure cooker soup recipes can help you get a healthy and delicious meal on your table fast. Steam pressure builds up inside the sealed pot to achieve a high level of heat in a short period of time, which allows flavor to penetrate the food more deeply, tenderizing even the toughest cuts of meat. Ingredients that usually take a long time to prepare (such as dried black beans and barley) can be cooked in a fraction of the time.

Save energy

Electric pressure cookers are energy-efficient kitchen appliances. Pressure cooking allows you to prepare foods faster than conventional cooking methods like steaming and baking. The less time it takes to cook your meal, the less energy is required.

Safe and easy to operate

Unlike old-fashioned stovetop pressure cookers, the electric pressure cooker comes with several preset cooking functions designed to produce consistent cooking results. There are also many safety features that make it safe and easy to use. You can enjoy all the benefits of a pressure cooker with fewer risks of explosions or other unfortunate mishaps.

THE ANATOMY OF SOUP

Making a well-balanced soup traditionally requires a strategic approach to build flavors in stages, while you taste and adjust as you go. But with an electric pressure cooker, the ingredients are often cooked at the same time and transformed into their optimal texture as they impart flavors into the soup. To make a great bowl of soup, you'll need the following components:

Base

Most soups are created with water as the base, so the depth of flavor comes from the ingredients that are used. Hearty soups are often loaded with aromatics and flavorful ingredients, like smoked ham hock, onions, and garlic, which infuse the water with flavor and essentially produce their own stock as they cook. But you may want to use stock or broth in quick-cooking recipes to create more body and depth of flavor. In some cases, wine or beer may be added to enhance flavor. Since the electric pressure cooker provides a tight seal, liquid will not evaporate as it would on the stovetop, so the amount of liquid may be less than what you would expect from soup recipes made the traditional way.

Aromatics

Aromatics are vegetables that help impart flavors to soups and stews. Common aromatics include fennel, garlic, ginger, leeks, and onions. Most recipes call for sautéing the vegetables in a little olive oil or butter and letting them soften or caramelize before adding liquid; this is a critical step in creating more complex flavors in your base.

Vegetables

Vegetables help form the flavor and texture of soups and are sometimes the stars of the show. Starchy vegetables like potato, butternut squash, and pumpkin add a creamy texture when pureed, while fresh vegetables like corn, carrots, and parsnips lend their sweetness to savory soups. Leafy greens like kale and Swiss chard don't take long to cook and can be added to hearty meat-based soups during the last few minutes of cooking. Vegetables will quickly soften in an electric pressure cooker, so the timing involved in adding and cooking them is important in creating dishes with exceptional texture.

Protein

Proteins like meat, legumes, and seafood make soups more substantial, nutritious, and filling. The electric pressure cooker is perfect for tenderizing lean or tough cuts of meat, so incorporating them in the beginning of the cooking process helps create that juicy, fall-apart meat texture. Legumes also cook quickly (with and without presoaking), and canned beans are used in some cases for convenience. Keep in mind that seafood such as fish, shrimp, and shellfish can get overcooked and chewy if cooked under high pressure for too long, so many of my recipes will call for these ingredients to be added at the end.

Garnish

Garnishes are the finishing touches that add flavor and texture to soups, turning them from good to great and sometimes giving them a picture-perfect presentation. Common garnishes to consider are:

- Croutons
- Crumbled bacon
- Dollop of sour cream or Greek yogurt
- Fresh herbs such as parsley, chives, and cilantro
- Fresh lemon juice
- Grated or shredded cheese
- Toasted nuts and seeds
- Tortilla chips

ELECTRIC PRESSURE COOKER SAFETY

You may have memories of an old-fashioned pressure cooker making hissing noises on the stovetop, spewing water and steam and looking like it could explode at any time. Rest assured that today's modern, updated electric pressure cookers are light-years ahead of their antiquated counterparts. Electric pressure cookers are safe as long as you follow good practices.

Here are some important safety tips to keep in mind:

- There are three ways to release the built-up pressure inside the electric pressure cooker: natural release, quick release, and a combination of the two.
- Natural release allows the pressure to slowly vent on its own after the cooking cycle is complete. When the float valve drops, the cooker is no longer pressurized and the lid becomes removable. This can take up to 30 minutes, depending on how full the pot is.
- Quick release is when you vent the pressure rapidly after the cooking cycle is complete by manually turning the pressure release valve on the top of the electric pressure cooker from "Sealing" to "Venting."
- Some recipes will call for a combination of the two methods: natural release for a specific amount of time, and then a quick release of the remaining pressure.
- When doing a quick release, turn the pressure release valve using a wooden spoon, kitchen tongs, or silicone pot holder to avoid the hot steam or liquid spewing out from the valve touching your bare hands.
- Regardless of which release method you use, always make sure that the float valve has dropped completely before attempting to open the lid. If the lid is locked, do not try to force it open.
- Be sure to add enough liquid when you're pressure cooking. Electric pressure cookers require a certain amount of liquid to achieve the right pressure (some models require at least ½ cup to 1 cup of liquid). Since there is a wide range of models on the market, it's important to read the user manual and follow the manufacturer's instructions.
- Never fill the inner pot more than two-thirds full, as the electric pressure cooker requires a certain amount of free space to work properly. Most electric pressure cookers have a "Max" fill line on the inside of the inner pot for guidance.
- Make sure the pressure release valve is set to "Sealing" and the silicone sealing ring is installed correctly in the sealing ring rack before cooking. Otherwise, the pot will not come to pressure.

COOKING TIPS FOR HIGH ALTITUDE

All the recipes in this book were tested at sea level. But for those of you who live 3,000 feet or more above sea level, the cooking times will need to be adjusted to account for the higher altitude. The higher the elevation, the lower the boiling point, which means foods will be cooking at a lower temperature. To compensate for the lower cooking temperature when using your electric pressure cooker, increase the cooking time by 5 percent for every 1,000 feet above 2,000 feet elevation.

Here is a sample High Altitude Cooking Time Adjustment Chart:

ELEVATION	% INCREASE	MULTIPLY COOKING TIME IN RECIPE BY (ROUND TO THE NEAREST WHOLE MINUTE)	IF THE RECIPE CALLS FOR 20 MINUTES, THEN ADJUST THE TIME TO . . .
3,000 feet	5%	1.05	21 minutes
4,000 feet	10%	1.10	22 minutes
5,000 feet	15%	1.15	23 minutes
6,000 feet	20%	1.20	24 minutes
7,000 feet	25%	1.25	25 minutes
8,000 feet	30%	1.30	26 minutes
9,000 feet	35%	1.35	27 minutes
10,000 feet	40%	1.40	28 minutes

EQUIPMENT CHECKLIST

While the electric pressure cooker is the primary piece of equipment that will be used, consider having these kitchen tools handy:

Immersion blender

This is the best tool to easily puree soups right in your electric pressure cooker without having to transfer them to a separate blender. If you don't have an immersion blender, you can allow the soup to cool for a few minutes, and use a food processor or traditional blender to puree the soup in batches.

Trivets

These pronged metal contraptions are placed in the inner pot to keep your food off the bottom of the pot. This way, the food items are not fully submerged in the liquid. Some recipes will require the trivet for steaming.

Extra sealing rings

Over time, some strong flavors, such as those in Coconut Curried Butternut Squash Soup (page 37) and Hungarian-Style Goulash (page 167), may be absorbed by the sealing ring, which can cause the smell of meat and spices to transfer to lighter and flavor-neutral soups. The easiest way to avoid this is to have a few spare sealing rings so you can replace them if necessary.

Rimmed baking sheets

These are ideal for roasting vegetables and bones for stock, toasting nuts, or making croutons for garnishes.

Silicone pot holders

These protect your hands from getting burned while manually switching the pressure release valve for quick release or getting the hot inner pot out of the electric pressure cooker. Although you can use other types of pot holders, silicone is safer when working with hot liquids and gives a better grip when holding the thin edges of the pot.

Metal colander and/or fine-mesh strainer

A metal colander makes separating the solids a cinch, especially when making broths or stocks. A fine-mesh strainer is optional, but it's useful for removing the small bits and pieces if you like a very clear stock or broth.

Electric pressure cooker silicone lid

A silicone lid allows you to save leftovers in the inner pot and store it in the refrigerator. It is also perfect for taking a meal to a party or potluck without having to transfer it to a different container.

Glass lid

A glass lid lets you monitor the cooking process without losing moisture, which is ideal for when your cooker is in "Keep Warm" or "Sauté" mode, or when you're simmering or reheating your soup.

STOCKING YOUR PANTRY

The majority of recipes in this book are made using accessible, everyday ingredients that can be found in most grocery stores. I like to keep some staple ingredients stocked in my pantry so I can easily whip up a batch of soup for a quick lunch or last-minute weeknight dinner. The following ingredients are the building blocks for flavor and are found in a wide range of soup recipes, so they're particularly useful to have on hand.

Vegetables

Staples include carrots, celery, onions, and potatoes, which are always best fresh. Other hearty greens like kale, Swiss chard, and escarole are also good for adding to soups. You may wish to consider stocking some frozen vegetables, such as corn, spinach, and peas, for times when you want to make soups in a pinch.

Herbs

Fresh herbs like thyme, rosemary, parsley, and chives add a lot of flavor and freshness to otherwise bland soups. If a recipe calls for fresh herbs, you can substitute dried herbs if that's all you have. Use 1 teaspoon of dried herb for every 1 tablespoon of fresh herb called for in the recipe.

Spices

Consider stocking your pantry with cumin, paprika, chili powder, curry powder, turmeric, cayenne pepper, and black peppercorns. Just remember, it's important that your spices are not too old because they tend to lose their potency and flavor after sitting in the pantry for years.

Broth or stock

Some soup recipes call for broth or stock as their base liquid. Homemade or store-bought versions both work well. See chapter 2 to learn how to create your own broth or stock, which can provide your soups with more depth of flavor.

Grains and legumes

Grains and legumes can be cooked in the electric pressure cooker in a fraction of the time it would take to cook them on the stovetop. These include barley, rice, quinoa, and farro. Dried legumes such as lentils, split peas, black beans, pinto beans, and black-eyed peas are also cook well in the electric pressure cooker, with or without presoaking. Keep some canned beans on hand for when you're pressed for time.

Thickening agents

Cornstarch and flour are often used to achieve thicker texture in soups. Dairy products such as heavy cream, milk, and sour cream can be used to add creaminess, but since dairy products have a tendency to curdle when they're cooked under pressure, be sure to add them *after* cooking.

BROTH: HOMEMADE VS. STORE-BOUGHT

Homemade broth tends to be more economical and flavorful, healthier, and free of preservatives. While homemade broth is my favorite in terms of taste, store-bought broth is a great shortcut I love to use when I'm short on time. It's convenient and accessible, so I keep a good amount of store-bought stock in my pantry. These days, grocery stores offer a wide variety of good-quality broths, including bone broths and organic broths as well as low-sodium varieties. If you do decide to use store-bought broth, try to find ones that are low in sodium or, even better, sodium-free. Also, since the broth imparts flavors to the soup, be sure to choose one with a base flavor you like.

STORING AND REHEATING SOUP

Homemade soup is the perfect make-ahead meal since it generally keeps well in the refrigerator or freezer. Most of the recipes in this cookbook store well, especially bean soups, stews, and broth-based soups. Some cream-based soups lose their smooth consistency after freezing and thawing, so an option would be to leave out the dairy when you're cooking and add it in after you have thawed and reheated the soup. Soups with pasta and noodles also tend to soak up the liquid and become mushy when made ahead and reheated. It's best to cook the pasta separately and stir it in when you are reheating the soup.

As a rule of thumb, soups kept in airtight containers will keep in the refrigerator for up to four days and in the freezer for up to three months for best quality. Let the soup cool before placing it in the refrigerator or freezer. You can speed up the cooling process by setting the pot of soup in a bath of ice water in the sink. Once it's cooled, ladle it into smaller, heavy-duty plastic (BPA-free) containers or freezer-safe mason jars and label them with the content and date the soup was made. If you plan to freeze it, be sure to leave at least 1 inch of space between the soup and the lid to allow for liquid expansion.

To reheat soup in the electric pressure cooker, you can use the "Sauté" mode. Alternatively, you can gently reheat soup in a large pot over medium-low heat on the stove or in a microwave-safe bowl in the microwave until warmed through. For frozen soup, let it thaw in the refrigerator before reheating. Add a splash of water or broth if it is too thick.

ABOUT THE RECIPES

The recipes in this book are organized by soup type, such as vegetarian soups, poultry soups, and hearty meat soups and stews. Included are classics that you already know and love as well as more modern versions with a refreshing twist. I have included a wide variety of soups that cater to different types of dietary requirements. Look out for the following labels:

- **45 MINUTES OR LESS:** can be completed in less than 45 minutes, including preparation and cooking time.
- **DAIRY-FREE:** do not contain any cow's-milk products or ingredients, which makes them suitable for those who want to eliminate dairy products from their diet.
- **FREEZER-FRIENDLY:** good for freezing and reheating.

- **GLUTEN-FREE:** do not have any grains that contain gluten such as wheat, barley, or rye. That said, some ingredients, like canned vegetables, sauces, and seasonings, may contain trace amounts of gluten from processing, so if you have any doubts, be sure to check the ingredients label.
- **VEGAN:** do not contain animal products, which also make them vegetarian-friendly. Some recipes will include variations and tips on substituting ingredients to make the soup dairy-free, gluten-free, or vegan.

A note on cooking times:

All of the recipes in this book were developed using a standard six-quart electric pressure cooker (Instant Pot® Duo). When you set the pressure cooking time on the appliance, it does not account for the time it takes for the unit to come to pressure. So, if the recipe calls for 10 minutes at high pressure, the total cooking time may be 25 minutes to account for the pressurizing time, plus extra time to depressurize (i.e., release) at the end of cooking. Be sure to factor in that time when planning your meals; at the top of each recipe, "pressurization time" refers to the time it takes the unit to come to pressure, and "release" refers the time it takes the unit to depressurize. Note that the amount of time it takes to come to pressure may be different between appliances, depending on the size of the pot and the temperature of the ingredients.

If you decide to double or halve a recipe, there's no need to change the cooking time. But be mindful of the volume of ingredients to make sure you have enough liquid and do not overfill the pot.

I recommend following the ingredients and instructions closely for the best results. Once you become more familiar with the process and cooking times, I hope you will use these recipes as a starting point for creating your own flavors based on your preferences while experimenting with whatever ingredients you have on hand. Let's get started!

CHAPTER 2

BROTHS AND STOCKS

Broths and stocks are key building blocks for soups, stews, gravies, and other dishes. Once you make a broth or stock in the electric pressure cooker, you may never go back to making it on a stovetop or in a slow cooker again.

Although the terms "stock" and "broth" are often used interchangeably and the techniques for making both are similar, there is a small difference that sets them apart. Stock is made by simmering bones in water, which creates a rich liquid with more body and depth. The collagen extracted from the bones during simmering also gives stock a slightly gelatinous texture. Sometimes, the bones are roasted before simmering, which makes for an even richer stock with a dark color (although roasting is not essential). Broth, on the other hand, is made by simmering meat (sometimes with bones as well), vegetables, and aromatics in water for a relatively short amount of time. Broth tends to be light and flavorful, at times requiring some light seasoning. Both broth and stock can be used as bases for all kinds of recipes, so you may want to store or freeze them unseasoned.

When you're making broths or stocks, it will take longer for the electric pressure cooker to build pressure because of the large amount of liquids that must be heated to a boil. To cut the time, use hot water or start warming the liquids using the "Sauté" mode as you prepare the rest of the ingredients.

VEGETABLE BROTH

Vegetable broth is a kitchen staple. This homemade version is hearty enough to enjoy alone as soup, but it also works perfectly as a base in your favorite recipe. It's a good way to put any leftover vegetables and herbs to use. I like to keep a container in my freezer so I can save the vegetable trimmings from other meals. Once the container gets full, I know it's time to make a batch of vegetable broth!

MAKES: 8 CUPS
PREP TIME: 5 MINUTES
PRESSURIZATION TIME:
16 MINUTES
COOK TIME: 15 MINUTES ON "MANUAL" MODE UNDER HIGH PRESSURE
RELEASE: NATURAL RELEASE FOR 5 MINUTES, THEN QUICK RELEASE
TOTAL TIME: 41 MINUTES

1 onion, quartered

3 carrots, coarsely chopped

2 celery stalks, coarsely chopped

3 garlic cloves, whole and unpeeled

1 tablespoon tomato paste

2 thyme sprigs

3 parsley sprigs

2 bay leaves

2 to 3 cups vegetable scraps (optional)

8 cups water

1. Place all of the ingredients in the inner pot of the pressure cooker and stir to combine.

2. Secure the lid. Select the "Manual" mode, and set the cooking time for 15 minutes under High Pressure. When the cooking cycle is complete, natural release for 5 minutes, then quick release any remaining steam.

3. Pour the broth through a colander into a large heat-safe bowl, and discard the solids. Let the broth cool, then store it in the refrigerator for up to a week or in the freezer for up to 3 months.

TIP: Some good vegetable scraps to use include carrot peels, green parts from leeks, mushroom stems, and celery ends. Certain vegetables and herbs can overpower your broth, so avoid starchy vegetables or those with assertive flavors such as Brussels sprouts, broccoli, bell peppers, and cilantro. Peeling vegetables is optional as long as you scrub or rinse them well.

If you have time, try roasting the onion, carrots, celery, and garlic on a baking sheet drizzled with olive oil in a 425°F oven for 30 minutes until the vegetables are caramelized, before using them in the broth. It will change the flavor of the broth and give it an incredible richness.

Per Serving (1 cup): Calories: 19; Protein: 1g; Fat: 0g; Saturated Fat: 0g; Carbohydrates: 4g; Sugar: 2g; Sodium: 23mg; Fiber: 1g

MUSHROOM BROTH

For a change of pace from the usual vegetable broth, make this hearty mushroom-infused version. It's packed with earthy, savory flavors that add a "meatiness" to it. I especially like using this full-bodied and complex broth in my favorite vegetable soups, stews, and risotto recipes.

MAKES: 8 CUPS

PREP TIME: 5 MINUTES

SAUTÉ TIME: 5 MINUTES

PRESSURIZATION TIME: 16 MINUTES

COOK TIME: 10 MINUTES ON "MANUAL" MODE UNDER HIGH PRESSURE

RELEASE: QUICK RELEASE

TOTAL TIME: 36 MINUTES

---

1 tablespoon olive oil

1 pound white button mushrooms, quartered

1 onion, quartered

3 garlic cloves, whole and unpeeled

4 thyme sprigs

8 cups water

1. Select the "Sauté" mode on the electric pressure cooker. Heat the olive oil and cook the mushrooms for 5 minutes, or until they start to release some moisture. Turn off the "Sauté" mode.

2. Add the onion, garlic, thyme, and water, and stir to combine.

3. Secure the lid. Select the "Manual" mode, and set the cooking time for 10 minutes under High Pressure. When the cooking cycle is complete, quick release any remaining steam.

4. Pour the broth through a colander into a large heat-safe bowl, and discard the solids. Let the broth cool, then store it in the refrigerator for up to a week or in the freezer for up to 3 months.

TIP: To add more dimension to this mushroom broth's flavor, use a mixture of fresh or dried mushrooms such as porcini, shiitake, cremini, or oyster.

Per Serving (1 cup): Calories: 25; Protein: 0g; Fat: 1g; Saturated Fat: 0g; Carbohydrates: 2g; Sugar: 1.5g; Sodium: 4mg; Fiber: 0g

CHICKEN BROTH

There really is no substitute for a proper homemade chicken broth. Traditionally, it would require hours of simmering to yield a mature broth—something that makes you say "wow" after one spoonful. This recipe aims to create that classic, complex chicken broth in under 90 minutes. Homemade chicken broth is great as a soup base and perfect for making gravies.

MAKES: 8 CUPS
PREP TIME: 5 MINUTES
PRESSURIZATION TIME:
17 MINUTES
COOK TIME: 45 MINUTES ON "MANUAL" MODE UNDER HIGH PRESSURE
RELEASE: NATURAL RELEASE FOR 15 MINUTES, THEN QUICK RELEASE
TOTAL TIME: 1 HOUR 22 MINUTES

1 (3- to 4-pound) whole chicken

1 onion, quartered

2 carrots, coarsely chopped

1 celery stalk, coarsely chopped

2 garlic cloves, whole and unpeeled

1 bay leaf

2 thyme sprigs

5 parsley sprigs

8 cups water

1. Place all of the ingredients in the inner pot of the pressure cooker and stir to combine.

2. Secure the lid. Select the "Manual" mode, and set the cooking time for 45 minutes under High Pressure. When the cooking cycle is complete, natural release for 15 minutes, then quick release any remaining steam.

3. Pour the broth through a colander into a large heat-safe bowl, and discard the solids. Skim the fat off if desired. Let the broth cool, then store it in the refrigerator for up to a week or in the freezer for up to 3 months.

TIP: Meat from the cooked chicken can be reserved for other uses. If you don't need to use the broth right away, refrigerate it until the fat solidifies on top for easy removal.

Per Serving (1 cup): Calories: 19; Protein: 1g; Fat: 0.5g; Saturated Fat: 0g; Carbohydrates: 2g; Sugar: 1g; Sodium: 37mg; Fiber: 0g

DASHI BROTH

One of my favorites, dashi is a basic broth commonly used in Japanese cooking. It serves as the base liquid for umami-rich dishes such as miso soup, udon and soba noodle soups, and even tempura dipping sauce. It only requires two ingredients: *kombu* (dried kelp) and *katsuobushi* (dried bonito flakes).

MAKES: 4 CUPS
PREP TIME: 20 MINUTES
SAUTÉ TIME: 15 MINUTES
TOTAL TIME: 35 MINUTES

1 (4-inch) piece kombu

4 cups water

1 cup loosely packed katsuobushi

1. Place the kombu and water in the inner pot of the pressure cooker and let it stand for 20 minutes.

2. Turn on the electric pressure cooker and select the "Sauté" mode. Once the water comes to a boil, remove the kombu with a slotted spoon. Add the katsuobushi and stir to combine. Turn off the "Sauté" mode and let it stand for 10 minutes.

3. Pour the broth through a colander into a large heat-safe bowl, and discard the katsuobushi. Let the broth cool, then store it in the refrigerator for up to a week or in the freezer for up to 3 months.

TIP: Kombu and katsuobushi can be found online or in the Asian food section of most major grocery stores. To make miso soup from the dashi broth, whisk 3 heaped tablespoons of white miso (fermented soybean paste) into 4 cups of dashi broth, and simmer with diced silken tofu and chopped scallions for about 5 minutes. Season with salt to taste.

Per Serving (1 cup): Calories: 2; Protein: 2g; Fat: 0g; Saturated Fat: 0g; Carbohydrates: 0g; Sugar: 0g; Sodium: 34mg; Fiber: 0g

CHICKEN STOCK

45 MINUTES OR LESS, DAIRY-FREE, FREEZER-FRIENDLY, GLUTEN-FREE

Making chicken stock is a good way to use up every part of a roasted or rotisserie chicken without letting the bones go to waste. Alternatively, you may have the bones and carcass from your holiday roasted turkey, with which you can use this method to make a flavorful roasted turkey stock. By extracting the flavors and nutrients from the bones, you're rewarded with a rich, flavorful stock that tastes like it has simmered all day.

MAKES: 8 CUPS

PREP TIME: 5 MINUTES

PRESSURIZATION TIME: 16 MINUTES

COOK TIME: 20 MINUTES ON "MANUAL" MODE UNDER HIGH PRESSURE

RELEASE: QUICK RELEASE

TOTAL TIME: 41 MINUTES

---

1 roasted or rotisserie chicken carcass with juices

1 onion, quartered

2 carrots, coarsely chopped

1 celery stalk, coarsely chopped

1 teaspoon apple cider vinegar

8 cups water

1. Place all of the ingredients in the inner pot of the pressure cooker and stir to combine.

2. Secure the lid. Select the "Manual" mode, and set the cooking time for 20 minutes under High Pressure. When the cooking cycle is complete, quick release any remaining steam.

3. Pour the stock through a colander into a large heat-safe bowl, and discard the solids. Let the stock cool, then store it in the refrigerator for up to a week or in the freezer for up to 3 months.

TIP: While it will be too subtle to taste, the acid in the vinegar helps extract nutrients from the bones to produce a heartier stock.

Per Serving (1 cup): Calories: 30; Protein: 6g; Fat: 0g; Saturated Fat: 0g; Carbohydrates: 1g; Sugar: 0g; Sodium: 70mg; Fiber: 0g

ROASTED BEEF BONE STOCK

DAIRY-FREE, FREEZER-FRIENDLY, GLUTEN-FREE

This beef bone stock is richly flavored and excellent for using in soups and other recipes, such as my Oxtail and Cabbage Soup (page 156) and Beef Bourguignon (page 154), or for sipping straight out of a mug. It's full of healthy nutrients, and this version gels beautifully due to its high levels of collagen. You can also use this exact method with pork bones.

MAKES: 8 TO 10 CUPS

PREP TIME: 15 MINUTES

PRESSURIZATION TIME: 20 MINUTES

COOK TIME: 1 HOUR 15 MINUTES ON "MANUAL" MODE UNDER HIGH PRESSURE

RELEASE: QUICK RELEASE

TOTAL TIME: 1 HOUR 50 MINUTES

---

3 pounds assorted beef bones, cut into smaller pieces

1 onion, quartered

1 carrot, coarsely chopped

1 celery stalk, coarsely chopped

1 rosemary sprig

2 bay leaves

1 teaspoon whole black peppercorns

1 tablespoon apple cider vinegar

8 to 10 cups water

1. Preheat the broiler and move the rack 3 inches from the heating source.

2. Arrange the bones and onion on a rimmed baking sheet and place them under the broiler. Roast for 15 minutes, turning halfway through, until the bones are browned and the onion is slightly charred.

3. Combine the roasted bones and onion with all of the other ingredients in the inner pot of the pressure cooker, making sure that the water is below the max line.

4. Secure the lid. Select the "Manual" mode, and set the cooking time for 1 hour 15 minutes (75 minutes) under High Pressure. When the cooking cycle is complete, quick release any remaining steam.

5. Pour the stock through a colander into a large heat-safe bowl, and discard the solids. Let the stock cool, then store it in the refrigerator for up to a week or in the freezer for up to 3 months.

TIP: Use a mix of beef soup bones, such as knuckles, marrow, ribs, and shanks. Ask the butcher for help in cutting them into 2-inch pieces so they can fit in the electric pressure cooker.

Per Serving (1 cup): Calories: 13; Protein: 2g; Fat: 0g; Saturated Fat: 0g; Carbohydrates: 1g; Sugar: 0g; Sodium: 67mg; Fiber: 0g

SHELLFISH STOCK

45 MINUTES OR LESS, DAIRY-FREE, FREEZER-FRIENDLY, GLUTEN-FREE

Next time you cook crab, shrimp, or lobster, don't discard the shells. They still pack a lot of flavor! When simmered with vegetables and herbs, they become the most delicious shellfish stock. You can use it as the base in almost any recipe that calls for fish stock or clam juice. It adds a great layer of flavor and hefty character to seafood soups and stews like my Cioppino (page 176), Thai-Inspired Tom Yum Seafood Soup (page 180), and Maryland-Style Crab Bisque (page 203), transforming them from average to incredible.

MAKES: 8 CUPS

PREP TIME: 5 MINUTES

PRESSURIZATION TIME:
15 MINUTES

COOK TIME: 10 MINUTES ON
"MANUAL" MODE UNDER HIGH
PRESSURE

RELEASE: NATURAL RELEASE FOR
15 MINUTES, THEN QUICK RELEASE

TOTAL TIME: 45 MINUTES

4 cups shellfish shells (from shrimp, lobster, crab, crawfish)

1 onion, quartered

1 carrot, coarsely chopped

1 celery stalk, coarsely chopped

1 bay leaf

5 parsley sprigs

8 cups water

1. Place all of the ingredients in the inner pot of the pressure cooker and stir to combine.

2. Secure the lid. Select the "Manual" mode, and set the cooking time for 10 minutes under High Pressure. When the cooking cycle is complete, natural release for 15 minutes, then quick release any remaining steam.

3. Pour the stock through a colander into a large heat-safe bowl, and discard the solids. Let the stock cool, then store it in the refrigerator for up to a week or in the freezer for up to 3 months.

TIP: Shellfish stock has a reddish hue due to the shells, so if you want a clear stock for a recipe, it's best to avoid it.

Per Serving (1 cup): Calories: 11; Protein: 0g; Fat: 0g; Saturated Fat: 0g; Carbohydrates: 1g; Sugar: 1g; Sodium: 12mg; Fiber: 0g

FISH STOCK

45 MINUTES OR LESS, DAIRY-FREE, FREEZER-FRIENDLY, GLUTEN-FREE

Homemade stock made from fish heads, bones, and trimmings is rich in flavor and nutrients. You can use it as the base for a variety of seafood recipes from Brazilian-Inspired Fish Stew (Moqueca) (page 199) to Salmon Chowder (page 197) to Classic French-Style Bouillabaisse (page 178). If I'm in the mood for a fish soup, I'll ask the fishmonger to fillet a few small fish and save the bones for me. Once the stock is done and strained, I'll cook the fillet in the simmering stock for a simple yet delicious soup.

MAKES: 8 CUPS

PREP TIME: 5 MINUTES

PRESSURIZATION TIME: 15 MINUTES

COOK TIME: 10 MINUTES "MANUAL" MODE UNDER HIGH PRESSURE

RELEASE: NATURAL RELEASE FOR 15 MINUTES, THEN QUICK RELEASE

TOTAL TIME: 45 MINUTES

---

2 pounds fish heads, trimmings, and bones (gills and skin removed)

1 onion, quartered

2 carrots, coarsely chopped

1 celery stalk, coarsely chopped

1 bay leaf

5 parsley sprigs

8 cups water

½ cup dry white wine (optional)

1. Place all of the ingredients in the inner pot of the pressure cooker and stir to combine.

2. Secure the lid. Select the "Manual" mode, and set the cooking time for 10 minutes under High Pressure. When the cooking cycle is complete, natural release for 15 minutes, then quick release any remaining steam.

3. Pour the stock through a colander into a large heat-safe bowl, and discard the solids. Let the stock cool, then store it in the refrigerator for up to a week or in the freezer for up to 3 months.

TIP: The best fish bones to use for making this stock are ones from mild, lean whitefish like halibut, cod, or flounder. As a general rule, you'll want to avoid salmon, mackerel, or other oily fish since their strong flavor will likely overpower your finished dish.

Per Serving (1 cup): Calories: 32; Protein: 5g; Fat: 0g; Saturated Fat: 0g; Carbohydrates: 1g; Sugar: 1g; Sodium: 77mg; Fiber: 0g

CHAPTER 3

VEGETABLE SOUPS

The recipes in this section celebrate seasonal produce at the peak of its flavor, from pureed soups such as Spring Pea and Mint Soup (page 30) and Fresh Corn Soup (page 31), to hearty classics like Broccoli and Cheese Soup (page 34) and Butternut Squash and Apple Soup (page 40). With the convenience of frozen vegetables picked at their prime, you can enjoy some of these soups all year long.

Cooking vegetable soups in the electric pressure cooker produces consistent results with no loss of flavor, texture, or authenticity. You will notice that a lot of recipes in this section require quick release. This will stop the cooking process to prevent overcooking the vegetables, and it will keep the colors of the vegetables from losing their vibrancy. One thing to note: Whenever a recipe calls for a meat broth, feel free to substitute vegetable broth for a vegetarian or vegan option.

< Spring Pea and Mint Soup, page 30

FRENCH ONION SOUP

FREEZER-FRIENDLY, GLUTEN-FREE

French Onion Soup feels like a bistro staple, but it's actually not at all difficult to make a quick version at home. The onions require some time to caramelize, but it's worth the effort so that the resulting rich beef broth is infused with the flavors of the sweet sautéed onions. As a garnish, a thick slice of toasted French baguette loaded with melted Gruyère takes this soup over the top!

SERVES: 6

PREP TIME: 5 MINUTES

SAUTÉ TIME: 15 MINUTES

PRESSURIZATION TIME:
12 MINUTES

COOK TIME: 20 MINUTES ON "MANUAL" MODE UNDER HIGH PRESSURE

RELEASE: NATURAL RELEASE FOR 15 MINUTES, THEN QUICK RELEASE

TOTAL TIME: 1 HOUR 7 MINUTES

---

4 tablespoons unsalted butter

6 large yellow onions, thinly sliced

4 garlic cloves, minced

⅓ cup dry sherry or white wine (optional)

4 thyme sprigs

1 bay leaf

1 tablespoon Worcestershire sauce

6 cups Roasted Beef Bone Stock (page 19) or store-bought unsalted beef broth

Salt

Freshly ground black pepper

1. Turn on the electric pressure cooker and select the "Sauté" mode. Melt the butter and cook the onions and garlic for 13 minutes, or until the onions begin to caramelize, stirring occasionally. Add the sherry (if using) and simmer for 2 minutes. Turn off the "Sauté" mode.

2. Add the thyme, bay leaf, Worcestershire sauce, and beef stock, and stir to combine.

3. Secure the lid. Select the "Manual" mode, and set the cooking time for 20 minutes under High Pressure. When the cooking cycle is complete, natural release for 15 minutes, then quick release any remaining steam.

4. Remove and discard the thyme sprigs and bay leaves.

5. Season with salt and pepper to taste.

TIP: French onion soup is traditionally served with broiled cheese toast. To serve, ladle it into oven-safe serving bowls or ramekins. Place a 1-inch slice of French baguette on top of the soup and sprinkle it evenly with 2 tablespoons of grated Gruyère. Place the bowls on a rimmed baking sheet and broil until cheese is melted and golden brown.

Per Serving: Calories: 148; Protein: 4g; Fat: 8g; Saturated Fat: 5g; Carbohydrates: 16g; Sugar: 6.5g; Sodium: 110mg; Fiber: 2.5g

CREAM OF MUSHROOM SOUP

45 MINUTES OR LESS, GLUTEN-FREE

Just about any kind of mushroom can be used in this recipe. I find that a mix of fresh and dried mushrooms, such as fresh cremini and dried porcini, produce the best flavor. You can serve this soup on its own or use it as a base for sauces, casseroles, or other recipes that call for cream of mushroom soup.

SERVES: 6

PREP TIME: 5 MINUTES

SAUTÉ TIME: 5 MINUTES

PRESSURIZATION TIME: 10 MINUTES

COOK TIME: 5 MINUTES ON "MANUAL" MODE UNDER HIGH PRESSURE

RELEASE: QUICK RELEASE

TOTAL TIME: 25 MINUTES

1 tablespoon olive oil

2 shallots, diced

2 garlic cloves, minced

½ cup sherry or dry white wine

1½ pounds white button mushrooms or any mix of mushrooms, sliced

3 thyme sprigs

1 teaspoon Worcestershire sauce

4 cups Vegetable Broth (page 14) or store-bought unsalted vegetable broth

2 tablespoons cornstarch

1 cup heavy (whipping) cream

Salt

Freshly ground black pepper

1. Turn on the electric pressure cooker and select the "Sauté" mode. Heat the olive oil and cook the shallots and garlic for 2 minutes, or until the shallots are soft. Add the sherry and simmer for 2 minutes. Turn off the "Sauté" mode.

2. Add the mushrooms, thyme, Worcestershire sauce, and broth, and stir to combine.

3. Secure the lid. Select the "Manual" mode, and set the cooking time for 5 minutes under High Pressure. When the cooking cycle is complete, quick release any remaining steam.

4. Remove and discard the thyme sprigs.

5. In a separate bowl, whisk together the cornstarch and heavy cream.

6. Select the "Sauté mode and bring the soup to a simmer. Then, add the cornstarch mixture and stir for 1 minute, or until the soup has thickened. Turn the electric pressure cooker off.

7. Season with salt and pepper to taste.

TIP: Switch up the flavors of the soup with rosemary, oregano, or tarragon in place of thyme. For a vegan or dairy-free version, you can substitute a milk alternative, such as almond milk or cashew milk, for the heavy cream, as long as it is unflavored and unsweetened.

Per Serving: Calories: 229; Protein: 6g; Fat: 17g; Saturated Fat: 9.5g; Carbohydrates: 12g; Sugar: 4.5g; Sodium: 112mg; Fiber: 1g

30 CLOVES OF GARLIC SOUP

45 MINUTES OR LESS

This recipe uses three heads of garlic, which yield about 30 cloves. It may sound like a recipe for warding off vampires, but once the garlic is roasted, the pungent flavor becomes much more mellow. While "roasting" garlic in the electric pressure cooker doesn't produce caramelization the way slow roasting in the oven does, the garlic cloves do become perfectly tender and sweet, so I can heartily recommend this method for use in this soup recipe. If you prefer, you can roast your garlic in the oven or on a grill.

SERVES: 6
PREP TIME: 5 MINUTES
SAUTÉ TIME: 2 MINUTES
PRESSURIZATION TIME:
12 MINUTES
COOK TIME: 17 MINUTES ON "MANUAL" MODE UNDER HIGH PRESSURE
RELEASE: QUICK RELEASE
TOTAL TIME: 36 MINUTES

1 cup water

3 garlic heads, halved

1 tablespoon olive oil

½ teaspoon salt, plus more to taste

2 tablespoons unsalted butter

2 onions, sliced

3 thyme sprigs

1 bay leaf

2 slices day-old rustic bread, torn into small pieces

4 cups Chicken Broth (page 16) or Vegetable Broth (page 14) or store-bought unsalted broth vegetable broth

½ cup half-and-half

1 tablespoon fresh lemon juice

Freshly ground black pepper

1. Place a trivet in the bottom of the electric pressure cooker and add the water. Cut ¼ inch off the top of the garlic heads to expose the cloves. Arrange the garlic on the trivet, cut-side up. Drizzle the bulbs with olive oil and sprinkle them with the ½ teaspooon salt.

2. Secure the lid. Select the "Manual" mode, and set the cooking time for 10 minutes under High Pressure. When the cooking cycle is complete, quick release any remaining steam. Using tongs, carefully remove the garlic bulbs and trivet, and pour out the hot water. Squeeze out the softened garlic cloves into a small bowl and discard the skin.

3. Select the "Sauté" mode. Melt the butter and cook the onions for 2 minutes, or until the onions are soft. Turn off the "Sauté" mode. Add the garlic cloves, thyme, bay leaf, bread, and broth, and stir to combine.

4. Secure the lid. Select the "Manual" mode again, and set the cooking time for 7 minutes under High Pressure. When the cooking cycle is complete, quick release any remaining steam.

5. Remove and discard the thyme sprigs and bay leaf.

6. Using an immersion blender, traditional blender, or food processor, blend the soup until smooth.

7. Stir in the half-and-half and lemon juice. Season with salt and pepper to taste.

TIP: If you don't have day-old bread on hand, arrange slices of fresh bread into a single layer on a rimmed baking sheet and bake in a 350°F oven for 15 minutes, or until toasted and dry but not browned.

Per Serving: Calories: 176; Protein: 6g; Fat: 8.5g; Saturated Fat: 4g; Carbohydrates: 17g; Sugar: 3.5g; Sodium: 404mg; Fiber: 1g

POTATO LEEK SOUP

45 MINUTES OR LESS, GLUTEN-FREE

If you're looking for comfort in a bowl, this rich and satisfying soup will warm you up. Leeks lend a distinct, subtle flavor, while the high starch content of russet potatoes helps thicken the soup and make it perfectly creamy. This recipe keeps things simple—you'll wonder how just a few basic ingredients could possibly yield such a flavorful soup.

SERVES: 6

PREP TIME: 5 MINUTES

SAUTÉ TIME: 2 MINUTES

PRESSURIZATION TIME: 12 MINUTES

COOK TIME: 7 MINUTES ON "MANUAL" MODE UNDER HIGH PRESSURE

RELEASE: QUICK RELEASE

TOTAL TIME: 26 MINUTES

2 tablespoons unsalted butter

4 large leeks (white and light green parts only), thinly sliced

2 garlic cloves, coarsely chopped

3 russet potatoes, diced

3 thyme sprigs

1 bay leaf

5 cups Vegetable Broth (page 14) or Chicken Broth (page 16) or store-bought unsalted chicken or vegetable broth

½ cup half-and-half

Salt

Freshly ground black pepper

1. Turn on the electric pressure cooker and select the "Sauté" mode. Melt the butter and cook the leeks and garlic for 2 minutes. Turn off the "Sauté" mode.

2. Add the potatoes, thyme, bay leaf, and broth, and stir to combine.

3. Secure the lid. Select the "Manual" mode, and set the cooking time for 7 minutes under High Pressure. When the cooking cycle is complete, quick release any remaining steam.

4. Remove and discard the thyme sprigs and bay leaf.

5. Using an immersion blender, traditional blender, or food processor, blend the soup until smooth.

6. Stir in the half-and-half and season with salt and pepper to taste.

TIP: Since leeks are grown in sandy soil, they need a good cleaning before you use them in recipes. After trimming the roots and green parts, slice the leeks in half lengthwise and rinse the grit from between the inner layers of the vegetables before slicing them.

For a vegan or dairy-free version, you can substitute olive oil for the butter and a milk alternative of your choice for the half-and-half as long as it is unflavored and unsweetened.

Per Serving: Calories: 207; Protein: 7g; Fat: 6g; Saturated Fat: 4g; Carbohydrates: 33g; Sugar: 5g; Sodium: 136mg; Fiber: 2.5g

CREAMY ASPARAGUS SOUP

45 MINUTES OR LESS, GLUTEN-FREE

This fresh, brightly flavored soup is as comforting as it is elegant. It's one of my favorite soups to make in the spring when I can find the freshest bunch of asparagus. If you're able to source some white asparagus, it would make for a fun variation to use to surprise your dinner guests. A squeeze of lemon juice stirred in at the end of cooking really makes the soup shine, so don't skip it.

SERVES: 6

PREP TIME: 5 MINUTES

SAUTÉ TIME: 2 MINUTES

PRESSURIZATION TIME: 10 MINUTES

COOK TIME: 5 MINUTES ON "MANUAL" MODE UNDER HIGH PRESSURE

RELEASE: QUICK RELEASE

TOTAL TIME: 22 MINUTES

1 tablespoon unsalted butter

1 medium leek (white and light green parts only), thinly sliced

1½ pounds asparagus, trimmed

4 cups Vegetable Broth (page 14) or Chicken Broth (page 16) or store-bought unsalted chicken or vegetable broth

½ cup heavy (whipping) cream

1 tablespoon fresh lemon juice

Salt

Freshly ground black pepper

1. Turn on the electric pressure cooker and select the "Sauté" mode. Melt the butter and cook the leek for 2 minutes. Turn off the "Sauté" mode. Add the asparagus and broth, and stir to combine.

2. Secure the lid. Select the "Manual" mode, and set the cooking time for 5 minutes under High Pressure. When the cooking cycle is complete, quick release any remaining steam.

3. Using an immersion blender, traditional blender, or food processor, blend the soup until smooth.

4. Stir in the heavy cream and lemon juice. Season with salt and pepper to taste.

TIP: Garlic baguette chips are a delicious garnish for this soup. To make them, cut a loaf of French baguette into ¼-inch slices. Combine ¼ cup of melted unsalted butter, two coarsely chopped garlic cloves, and ¼ teaspoon of salt in a small bowl. Brush the butter mixture over the baguette slices with a pastry brush and place them on a baking sheet. Bake at 350°F for 10 minutes, or until toasted and golden brown. Remove the chips from oven and let them cool completely on the baking sheet before serving.

Per Serving: Calories: 119; Protein: 4g; Fat: 9.5g; Saturated Fat: 6g; Carbohydrates: 6g; Sugar: 2.5g; Sodium: 99mg; Fiber: 1.5g

SPRING PEA AND MINT SOUP

45 MINUTES OR LESS, FREEZER-FRIENDLY, GLUTEN-FREE

Fresh peas and mint are a classic combination and definitely a match made in soup heaven. This soup is great as a first course on its own or as a more substantial lunch or dinner served with some crusty whole-grain bread. It's fresh, light, and delicious served hot or chilled. You can use crème fraîche, sour cream, or a dollop of Greek yogurt stirred into the soup.

SERVES: 4

PREP TIME: 5 MINUTES

SAUTÉ TIME: 2 MINUTES

PRESSURIZATION TIME:
10 MINUTES

COOK TIME: 5 MINUTES ON
"MANUAL" MODE UNDER HIGH
PRESSURE

RELEASE: QUICK RELEASE

TOTAL TIME: 22 MINUTES

---

1 tablespoon olive oil

2 small shallots, sliced

4 cups shelled fresh or frozen peas

4 cups Vegetable Broth (page 14) or Chicken Broth (page 16) or store-bought unsalted chicken or vegetable broth

2 tablespoons freshly chopped parsley

¼ cup freshly chopped mint leaves

Salt

Freshly ground black pepper

1. Turn on the electric pressure cooker and select the "Sauté" mode. Heat the olive oil and cook the shallots for 2 minutes, or until they are soft. Turn off the "Sauté" mode.

2. Add the peas and broth, and stir to combine.

3. Secure the lid. Select the "Manual" mode, and set the cooking time for 5 minutes under High Pressure. When the cooking cycle is complete, quick release any remaining steam.

4. Add the parsley and mint, and blend the soup until smooth using an immersion blender, traditional blender, or food processor.

5. Season with salt and pepper to taste.

TIP: If you're using frozen peas, add them to the pot and follow the instructions provided. There is no need to increase the cook time because the peas will defrost as the pot is coming to pressure, though it will take slightly longer than if you're using fresh peas.

Per Serving: Calories: 179; Protein: 11g; Fat: 4g; Saturated Fat: 0.5g; Carbohydrates: 25g; Sugar: 10g; Sodium: 136mg; Fiber: 9g

FRESH CORN SOUP

45 MINUTES OR LESS, FREEZER-FRIENDLY, GLUTEN-FREE

With a short list of ingredients, this unassuming, perfectly seasoned vegetable soup is something you'll want to make again and again. It highlights freshly shucked corn kernels, while the cobs are used to make its broth, so all the milky sweetness of the corn is front and center.

SERVES: 6

PREP TIME: 5 MINUTES

SAUTÉ TIME: 2 MINUTES

PRESSURIZATION TIME: 12 MINUTES

COOK TIME: 7 MINUTES ON "MANUAL" MODE UNDER HIGH PRESSURE

RELEASE: QUICK RELEASE

TOTAL TIME: 26 MINUTES

---

2 tablespoons unsalted butter

3 shallots, diced

Kernels of 6 ears freshly shucked corn, cob reserved

6 cups Chicken Broth (page 16) or store-bought unsalted chicken broth

Salt

Freshly ground black pepper

1. Turn on the electric pressure cooker and select the "Sauté" mode. Melt the butter and cook the shallots for 2 minutes, or until they are soft. Turn off the "Sauté" mode.

2. Add the corn kernels, cobs, and broth, and stir to combine.

3. Secure the lid. Select the "Manual" mode, and set the cooking time for 7 minutes under High Pressure. When the cooking cycle is complete, quick release any remaining steam.

4. Remove and discard the cobs, and reserve about 1 cup of corn kernels.

5. Using an immersion blender, traditional blender, or food processor, blend the soup until smooth.

6. Stir in the reserved corn and season with salt and pepper to taste.

TIP: If you have a high-powered blender, use it in this recipe for a perfectly smooth soup. You can also pass it through a fine-mesh strainer before serving. Give it a taste before taking this extra step—you might actually enjoy the texture, which lends a more rustic character to this delicious soup. For a garnish, chop up some fresh chives and sprinkle them on top.

Per Serving: Calories: 168; Protein: 7g; Fat: 5.5g; Saturated Fat: 3g; Carbohydrates: 27g; Sugar: 10g; Sodium: 145mg; Fiber: 3g

POTATO AND CORN CHOWDER

45 MINUTES OR LESS, GLUTEN-FREE

Potatoes are a total comfort, and when you add bacon to the equation, you know it's going to be a winner. This chowder can be made any night of the week, even on a busy day. While it can easily be served as a stand-alone entrée, pair the chowder with a side salad and some crusty bread to make it a complete meal. Dinner's done in under 35 minutes.

SERVES: 6

PREP TIME: 5 MINUTES

SAUTÉ TIME: 8 MINUTES

PRESSURIZATION TIME:
10 MINUTES

COOK TIME: 10 MINUTES ON "MANUAL" MODE UNDER HIGH PRESSURE

RELEASE: QUICK RELEASE

TOTAL TIME: 33 MINUTES

---

4 bacon slices, diced

1 onion, diced

3 garlic cloves, minced

4 Yukon Gold or red potatoes, skin left on and diced

3 cups fresh or frozen corn kernels

2 thyme sprigs

4 cups Chicken Broth (page 16) or Vegetable Broth (page 14) or store-bought unsalted chicken or vegetable broth

1 tablespoon cornstarch

¾ cup half-and-half

Salt

Freshly ground black pepper

1. Turn on the electric pressure cooker and select the "Sauté" mode. Cook the bacon for 5 minutes, or until crisp. Retain about 1 tablespoon of fat in the pot. Transfer the bacon to a plate lined with paper towels and set aside.

2. Add the onion and garlic and cook for 2 minutes, or until the onion is soft. Turn off the "Sauté" mode.

3. Add the potatoes, corn, thyme, and broth, and stir to combine.

4. Secure the lid. Select the "Manual" mode, and set the cooking time for 10 minutes under High Pressure. When the cooking cycle is complete, quick release any remaining steam.

5. Remove and discard the thyme sprigs.

6. In a separate bowl, whisk together the cornstarch and half-and-half. Select the "Sauté" mode again and bring the soup to a simmer. Then, add the cornstarch mixture and stir for 1 minute, or until the soup has thickened. Turn the electric pressure cooker off.

7. Season with salt and pepper to taste.

TIP: For a lighter soup, substitute milk for the half-and-half. For a dairy-free version, you can substitute a milk alternative of your choice for the half-and-half as long as it is unflavored and unsweetened.

Per Serving: Calories: 271; Protein: 10g; Fat: 8.5g; Saturated Fat: 4g; Carbohydrates: 42g; Sugar: 9g; Sodium: 232mg; Fiber: 4g

TOMATO AND BASIL BISQUE

This bisque is a warming and luxurious soup that's simple to make and will have you coming back for more. A splash of heavy cream adds just enough richness without overpowering the flavor of the tomatoes.

SERVES: 6

PREP TIME: 5 MINUTES

SAUTÉ TIME: 2 MINUTES

PRESSURIZATION TIME: 10 MINUTES

COOK TIME: 10 MINUTES ON "MANUAL" MODE UNDER HIGH PRESSURE

RELEASE: QUICK RELEASE

TOTAL TIME: 27 MINUTES

1 tablespoon unsalted butter

1 onion, diced

4 garlic cloves, crushed

2 carrots, coarsely chopped

¼ teaspoon dried oregano

3 tablespoons tomato paste

3 (15-ounce) cans diced fire-roasted tomatoes

4 cups Vegetable Broth (page 14) or store-bought unsalted vegetable broth (or water)

½ cup fresh basil, chopped

½ cup heavy (whipping) cream

Salt

Freshly ground black pepper

Sugar (optional)

1. Turn on the electric pressure cooker and select the "Sauté" mode. Melt the butter and cook the onion and garlic for 2 minutes, or until the onion is soft. Turn off the "Sauté" mode.

2. Add the carrots, oregano, tomato paste, fire-roasted diced tomatoes with their juices, and broth.

3. Secure the lid. Select the "Manual" mode, and set the cooking time for 10 minutes under High Pressure. When the cooking cycle is complete, quick release any remaining steam.

4. Add the basil, and blend the soup until smooth using an immersion blender, traditional blender, or food processor.

5. Stir in the heavy cream and season with salt and pepper to taste. Depending on the ripeness of the tomatoes, if the soup is too acidic, season it with sugar (if using) to taste to balance the flavors.

TIP: If fresh tomatoes are in season, you can substitute 3 pounds of plum tomatoes for the canned tomatoes. To intensify their natural sweetness, place the halved tomatoes on a baking sheet drizzled with olive oil and roast them in a 450°F oven for 25 minutes, or until they are soft and caramelized around the edges.

Per Serving: Calories: 175; Protein: 4g; Fat: 9g; Saturated Fat: 6g; Carbohydrates: 19g; Sugar: 9.5g; Sodium: 531mg; Fiber: 5.5g

BROCCOLI AND CHEESE SOUP

45 MINUTES OR LESS, GLUTEN-FREE

It's hard not to love broccoli. All of its greenness just screams "good-for-you," even when it's paired with cheese. This soup is one part classic, one part unexpected, and all parts delicious. Because of the short cooking time, I love to make it for lunch or an easy weeknight dinner. This recipe jazzes up the classic with Gouda in addition to sharp cheddar, adding a nutty, buttery flavor that keeps everyone guessing.

SERVES: 6

PREP TIME: 5 MINUTES

SAUTÉ TIME: 3 MINUTES

PRESSURIZATION TIME: 10 MINUTES

COOK TIME: 1 MINUTE ON "MANUAL" MODE UNDER HIGH PRESSURE

RELEASE: QUICK RELEASE

TOTAL TIME: 19 MINUTES

2 tablespoons unsalted butter

1 onion, diced

4 cups coarsely chopped broccoli florets

1 cup shredded carrot

4 cups Chicken Broth (page 16) or Vegetable Broth (page 14) or store-bought unsalted chicken or vegetable broth

¼ cup cornstarch

2¼ cups milk

1½ cups grated sharp cheddar

1½ cups grated Gouda

Salt

Freshly ground black pepper

1. Turn on the electric pressure cooker and select the "Sauté" mode. Melt the butter and cook the onion for 2 minutes, or until soft. Turn off the "Sauté" mode.

2. Add the broccoli, carrot, and broth, and stir to combine.

3. Secure the lid. Select the "Manual" mode, and set the cooking time for 1 minute under High Pressure. When the cooking cycle is complete, quick release any remaining steam.

4. In a separate bowl, whisk together the cornstarch and milk. Select the "Sauté" mode and bring the soup to a simmer. Then, add the cornstarch mixture and stir for 1 minute, or until the soup has thickened. Stir in the sharp cheddar and Gouda until melted. Turn the electric pressure cooker off.

5. Season with salt and pepper to taste.

TIP: Experiment with different cheeses to suit your taste. Sharp cheddar provides a good base, but you can substitute other easy-to-melt cheeses such as pepper Jack, Monterey Jack, or Havarti for the Gouda.

Per Serving: Calories: 359; Protein: 21g; Fat: 24g; Saturated Fat: 14g; Carbohydrates: 46g; Sugar: 7.5g; Sodium: 556mg; Fiber: 2.5g

CAULIFLOWER SOUP

45 MINUTES OR LESS, GLUTEN-FREE

This velvety-smooth soup is more than a simple puree of cauliflower. Its texture is reminiscent of a classic potato soup—but without the starch, satisfying so many cravings and feeling just a touch indulgent. It's a great option for those who are on a low-carb or keto diet.

SERVES: 6

PREP TIME: 5 MINUTES

SAUTÉ TIME: 8 MINUTES

PRESSURIZATION TIME: 9 MINUTES

COOK TIME: 8 MINUTES ON "MANUAL" MODE UNDER HIGH PRESSURE

RELEASE: QUICK RELEASE

TOTAL TIME: 30 MINUTES

---

4 bacon slices, diced

1 tablespoon olive oil

3 shallots, sliced

2 celery stalks, diced

1 head cauliflower, cut into florets

3 cups Chicken Broth (page 16) or Vegetable Broth (page 14) or store-bought unsalted chicken or vegetable broth

½ cup half-and-half

Salt

Freshly ground black pepper

1. Turn on the electric pressure cooker and select the "Sauté" mode. Cook the bacon for 5 minutes, or until crisp. Transfer the bacon to a plate lined with paper towels and set aside.

2. Heat the olive oil and cook the shallots and celery for 3 minutes, or until the shallots are soft. Turn off the "Sauté" mode.

3. Add the cauliflower and broth, and stir to combine.

4. Secure the lid. Select the "Manual" mode, and set the cooking time for 8 minutes under High Pressure. When the cooking cycle is complete, quick release any remaining steam.

5. Using an immersion blender, traditional blender, or food processor, blend the soup until smooth.

6. Stir in the half-and-half and season with salt and pepper to taste. Garnish with bacon before serving.

TIP: Everything bagel croutons are a delicious garnish for this soup. To make them, combine two cubed plain bagels, 2 tablespoons of extra-virgin olive oil, and 2 tablespoons of everything bagel seasoning in a large baking sheet and toss till coated. Bake at 350°F for 10 to 15 minutes, or until toasted and golden brown. Remove the croutons from the oven and let them cool completely on the baking sheet before serving.

Per Serving: Calories: 179; Protein: 7g; Fat: 12g; Saturated Fat: 4g; Carbohydrates: 12g; Sugar: 6g; Sodium: 242mg; Fiber: 3g

COCONUT CURRIED BUTTERNUT SQUASH SOUP

Ever since I discovered how fast this butternut squash soup cooks in an electric pressure cooker, I've never gone back to making it on the stovetop. In fact, this method works so well, I make variations of this soup with kabocha or acorn squash. Despite the short cooking time, it produces an aromatic soup with a silky, creamy texture.

SERVES: 4

PREP TIME: 5 MINUTES

SAUTÉ TIME: 2 MINUTES

PRESSURIZATION TIME: 12 MINUTES

COOK TIME: 8 MINUTES ON "MANUAL" MODE UNDER HIGH PRESSURE

RELEASE: NATURAL RELEASE FOR 10 MINUTES, THEN QUICK RELEASE

TOTAL TIME: 37 MINUTES

1 tablespoon olive oil

2 shallots, sliced

2 garlic cloves, minced

1½ tablespoons curry powder

½ teaspoon ground cumin

5 cups butternut squash, peeled, seeded, and cubed

2 cups Vegetable Broth (page 14) or store-bought unsalted vegetable broth

1 cup coconut milk

Salt

Freshly ground black pepper

1. Turn on the electric pressure cooker and select the "Sauté" mode. Heat the olive oil and cook the shallots, garlic, curry powder, and cumin for 2 minutes, or until the shallots are soft and the spices are fragrant. Turn off the "Sauté" mode.

2. Add the squash and broth, and stir to combine.

3. Secure the lid. Select the "Manual" mode, and set the cooking time for 8 minutes under High Pressure. When the cooking cycle is complete, natural release for 10 minutes, then quick release any remaining steam.

4. Using an immersion blender, traditional blender, or food processor, blend the soup until smooth.

5. Stir in the coconut milk and season with salt and pepper to taste.

TIP: To give the soup a pop of freshness and crunch, you can garnish it with chopped chives and toasted pumpkin seeds. Adding an optional drizzle of sour cream also provides an extra layer of complexity.

Per Serving: Calories: 257; Protein: 4g; Fat: 16g; Saturated Fat: 11g; Carbohydrates: 30g; Sugar: 7g; Sodium: 30mg; Fiber: 6.5g

AUTUMN CARROT AND PARSNIP SOUP WITH CHERMOULA

Chermoula is a beautiful green pesto-like condiment that is used in North African cooking. It is traditionally used as a sauce with seafood, but can be also used as a marinade for meats or a sauce for vegetables. In this case, a spoonful of herbaceous chermoula brightens up this autumn-friendly soup and gives it a robust flavor. If you're short on time or want to simplify things further, feel free to skip the chermoula and just make the soup.

SERVES: 6

PREP TIME: 10 MINUTES

SAUTÉ TIME: 3 MINUTES

PRESSURIZATION TIME:
10 MINUTES

COOK TIME: 8 MINUTES ON
"MANUAL" MODE UNDER HIGH
PRESSURE

RELEASE: NATURAL RELEASE FOR
10 MINUTES, THEN QUICK RELEASE

TOTAL TIME: 41 MINUTES

FOR THE CHERMOULA

½ cup packed cilantro leaves

¼ cup packed parsley leaves

1 garlic clove, crushed

1 teaspoon ground cumin

1 teaspoon paprika

¼ teaspoon red pepper flakes

¼ cup olive oil

1 tablespoon fresh lemon juice

Salt

Freshly ground black pepper

FOR THE SOUP

2 tablespoons olive oil

1 onion, diced

2 garlic cloves, minced

1 tablespoon freshly grated ginger

1 teaspoon ground turmeric

¼ teaspoon ground cinnamon

Pinch cayenne pepper

4 carrots, peeled and diced

3 parsnips, diced

4 cups Vegetable Broth (page 14)
or store-bought unsalted
vegetable broth

1½ cups coconut milk

Salt

Freshly ground black pepper

1. Place all of the ingredients except salt and pepper in a blender or food processor and blend until the mixture is smooth. Add a teaspoon of water at a time to help with blending if necessary.

2. Season with salt and pepper to taste.

TO MAKE THE SOUP

3. Turn on the electric pressure cooker and select the "Sauté" mode. Heat the olive oil and cook the onion for 2 minutes, or until soft. Add the garlic, ginger, turmeric, cinnamon, and cayenne pepper and cook for 1 minute or until the spices are fragrant. Turn off the "Sauté" mode.

4. Add the carrots, parsnips, and broth, and stir to combine.

5. Secure the lid. Select the "Manual" mode, and set the cooking time for 8 minutes under High Pressure. When the cooking cycle is complete, natural release for 10 minutes, then quick release any remaining steam.

6. Using an immersion blender, traditional blender, or food processor, blend the soup until smooth. Add the coconut milk and season with salt and pepper to taste. Garnish with the chermoula before serving.

TIP: It's best to choose small- to medium-size parsnips, as the larger ones tend to have a bitter, woody core that will be tough and indigestible.

Per Serving: Calories: 330; Protein: 3g; Fat: 26g; Saturated Fat: 13g; Carbohydrates: 25g; Sugar: 8g; Sodium: 63mg; Fiber: 6g

BUTTERNUT SQUASH AND APPLE SOUP

Here's a soup that's smooth and creamy without being heavy, thanks to tart apples and a touch of cream to enrich the flavor. A topping of toasted spiced pepitas (shelled pumpkin seeds) adds a nice crunch, making it a wonderful, comforting autumn treat.

SERVES: 6

PREP TIME: 5 MINUTES

SAUTÉ TIME: 3 MINUTES

PRESSURIZATION TIME:
12 MINUTES

COOK TIME: 5 MINUTES ON "MANUAL" MODE UNDER HIGH PRESSURE

RELEASE: NATURAL RELEASE FOR 10 MINUTES, THEN QUICK RELEASE

TOTAL TIME: 35 MINUTES

---

1 tablespoon olive oil

1 onion, diced

3 garlic cloves, coarsely chopped

1 teaspoon freshly grated ginger

½ teaspoon ground cumin

½ teaspoon ground coriander

6 cups butternut squash, peeled, seeded, and cubed

2 Granny Smith apples, peeled, cored, and chopped

3 cups Vegetable Broth (page 14)

½ cup heavy (whipping) cream

Salt

Freshly ground black pepper

Toasted spiced pepitas (optional)

1. Turn on the electric pressure cooker and select the "Sauté" mode. Heat the olive oil and cook the onion for 2 minutes, or until soft. Add the garlic, ginger, cumin, and coriander and cook for 1 minute, or until the spices are fragrant. Turn off the "Sauté" mode.

2. Add the butternut squash, apples, and broth, and stir to combine.

3. Secure the lid. Select the "Manual" mode, and set the cooking time for 5 minutes under High Pressure. When the cooking cycle is complete, natural release for 10 minutes, then quick release any remaining steam.

4. Using an immersion blender, traditional blender, or food processor, blend the soup until smooth.

5. Stir in the heavy cream and season with salt and pepper to taste. Garnish with the pepitas (if using) before serving.

TIP: Butternut squash can be difficult to peel and cut open. If you prick the squash several times with a fork and microwave it for about 3 minutes, it will soften slightly, making it easier to handle.

Per Serving: Calories: 170; Protein: 3g; Fat: 9.5g; Saturated Fat: 5g; Carbohydrates: 21g; Sugar: 5g; Sodium: 24mg; Fiber: 3.5g

SPICED CARROT AND CASHEW SOUP

45 MINUTES OR LESS, DAIRY-FREE, FREEZER-FRIENDLY, GLUTEN-FREE, VEGAN

This soup elevates the traditional carrot and ginger soup with the addition of cashews, which is a great way to add luscious richness to the soup without using dairy. In fact, many pureed soup recipes in this book that require heavy cream or half-and-half as the thickening agent can be made dairy-free by adding cashews during cooking or cashew cream at the end.

SERVES: 4

PREP TIME: 5 MINUTES

SAUTÉ TIME: 3 MINUTES

PRESSURIZATION TIME:
12 MINUTES

COOK TIME: 8 MINUTES ON "MANUAL" MODE UNDER HIGH PRESSURE

RELEASE: NATURAL RELEASE FOR 10 MINUTES, THEN QUICK RELEASE

TOTAL TIME: 38 MINUTES

2 tablespoons olive oil

1 onion, chopped

2 garlic cloves, minced

1 tablespoon freshly grated ginger

1 teaspoon smoked paprika

1 teaspoon ground cumin

5 carrots, peeled and coarsely chopped

1 cup raw unsalted cashews

5 cups Vegetable Broth (page 14) or store-bought broth

Salt

Freshly ground black pepper

1. Turn on the electric pressure cooker and select the "Sauté" mode. Heat the olive oil and cook the onion for 2 minutes, or until soft. Add the garlic, ginger, paprika, and cumin and cook for 1 minute more. Turn off the "Sauté" mode.

2. Add the carrots, cashews, and broth, and stir to combine.

3. Secure the lid. Select the "Manual" mode, and set the cooking time for 8 minutes under High Pressure. When the cooking cycle is complete, natural release for 10 minutes, then quick release any remaining steam.

4. Using an immersion blender, traditional blender, or food processor, blend the soup until smooth. Season with salt and pepper to taste.

TIP: For a lusciously smooth soup, use a high-powered blender or pass the soup through a fine-mesh strainer to remove the bits and pieces.

Per Serving: Calories: 289; Protein: 7g; Fat: 19g; Saturated Fat: 3g; Carbohydrates: 23g; Sugar: 9g; Sodium: 88mg; Fiber: 5g

PUMPKIN SOUP WITH FENNEL AND LEEKS

Whenever I have leftover pumpkin puree, my first instinct is to turn it into a sweet dish, like a pumpkin spice granola or pumpkin pancakes. This easy soup recipe combines pumpkin puree with fresh fennel and leeks, transforming it into a savory, creamy soup with warm spicy notes and just the right amount of sweetness from the vegetables. It's essentially a steaming bowl of sunshine! If you've never had fennel before, this would be a great introduction to its sweet anise flavor.

SERVES: 4

PREP TIME: 5 MINUTES

SAUTÉ TIME: 3 MINUTES

PRESSURIZATION TIME:
10 MINUTES

COOK TIME: 5 MINUTES ON "MANUAL" MODE UNDER HIGH PRESSURE

RELEASE: NATURAL RELEASE FOR 5 MINUTES, THEN QUICK RELEASE

TOTAL TIME: 28 MINUTES

2 tablespoons olive oil

1 leek (white and light green parts only), thinly sliced

1 fennel bulb, fronds removed and thinly sliced

2 garlic cloves, coarsely chopped

2 teaspoons smoked paprika

½ teaspoon ground cumin

¼ teaspoon ground nutmeg

1 (15-ounce) can pumpkin puree

4 cups Vegetable Broth (page 14) or store-bought unsalted vegetable broth

2 tablespoons maple syrup

Salt

Freshly ground black pepper

1. Turn on the electric pressure cooker and select the "Sauté" mode. Heat the olive oil and cook the leek, fennel, and garlic for 3 minutes, or until the vegetables start to become soft. Turn off the "Sauté" mode.

2. Add the paprika, cumin, nutmeg, pumpkin puree, and broth, and stir to combine.

3. Secure the lid. Select the "Manual" mode, and set the cooking time for 5 minutes under High Pressure. When the cooking cycle is complete, natural release for 5 minutes, then quick release any remaining steam.

4. Using an immersion blender, traditional blender, or food processor, blend the soup until smooth.

5. Stir in the maple syrup and season with salt and pepper to taste.

TIP: Choose fennel with firm bulbs, bright green stalks, and fresh fronds. Typically, only the bulb is used in cooking and the fronds can be reserved for a garnish.

Per Serving: Calories: 180; Protein: 3g; Fat: 7.5g; Saturated Fat: 1g; Carbohydrates: 27g; Sugar: 15g; Sodium: 63mg; Fiber: 5.5g

CHAPTER 4

GRAIN AND BEAN SOUPS

The soups in this section incorporate beans and grains, which are wonderful for introducing vegetarian protein and fiber into your dinner rotation. The electric pressure cooker is great for making grain and bean soups because it's quicker than the stovetop method and much of the cooking time is hands-off. It certainly beats stirring a pot on the stove for hours!

Dried beans cook more evenly and don't split when they have been presoaked overnight. If you didn't plan ahead and soak the beans the night before, simply increase the pressure cooking time by 15 minutes and follow the pressure release instructions as directed. Alternately, you can quick-soak dried beans by covering them with water in a large saucepan, boiling them for 2 minutes, and letting them soak for an hour. Whole grains such as wheat berries, barley, rice, and farro are also well suited for the electric pressure cooker and don't require soaking at all.

Many recipes in this section refrigerate and freeze well, so it's a good idea to cook the full batch and save some for another meal. In fact, most bean soups develop better flavor and thicken quite nicely the second day of refrigeration. If you find that a soup is too thick, you can always thin it out with broth or water. On the other hand, rescuing a soup that's too thin can take hours of simmering. And while some of the recipes do include meat, you can make them vegetarian by omitting it.

< Pasta e Fagioli, page 60

CUBAN-INSPIRED BLACK BEAN SOUP

DAIRY-FREE, FREEZER-FRIENDLY, GLUTEN-FREE

There are a handful of classic soup recipes that I revisit throughout the years, and this is one of them. Take a look at the ingredient list, and you'll find that there's nothing fancy here. I love the smokiness that the ham hock gives, but you can certainly omit it to make it vegetarian friendly. The flavors and texture of this soup will develop with time, which is perfect as a meal-prep option for a busy week. Garnish it with sour cream, freshly chopped cilantro, and lime wedges.

SERVES: 6

PREP TIME: 5 MINUTES

SAUTÉ TIME: 4 MINUTES

PRESSURIZATION TIME: 12 MINUTES

COOK TIME: 20 MINUTES ON "MANUAL" MODE UNDER HIGH PRESSURE

RELEASE: NATURAL RELEASE FOR 15 MINUTES, THEN QUICK RELEASE

TOTAL TIME: 56 MINUTES

1 tablespoon olive oil

1 onion, diced

4 garlic cloves, minced

1 green bell pepper, seeded and diced

1 teaspoon ground cumin

1 teaspoon dried oregano

2 bay leaves

1 pound smoked ham hock

1 pound dried black beans, soaked overnight, rinsed, and drained

5 cups water

1 tablespoon red wine vinegar

Salt

Freshly ground black pepper

1. Turn on the electric pressure cooker and select the "Sauté" mode. Heat the olive oil and cook the onion, garlic, and bell pepper for 4 minutes, or until the vegetables are soft. Turn off the "Sauté" mode.

2. Add the cumin, oregano, bay leaves, smoked ham hock, beans, water, and vinegar, and stir to combine.

3. Secure the lid. Select the "Manual" mode, and set the cooking time for 20 minutes under High Pressure. When the cooking cycle is complete, natural release for 15 minutes, then quick release any remaining steam.

4. Remove and discard the bay leaves and ham hock.

5. Using an immersion blender, traditional blender, or food processor, partially blend the soup if a thicker consistency is desired.

6. Season with salt and pepper to taste.

TIP: If desired, you can remove the tender meat from the ham hock after cooking, chop it into smaller pieces, and add it to the soup.

As bean soups tend to thicken with time, I have used this leftover soup to make "refried" beans by simmering it on low until it becomes less soupy, then further breaking down the beans with a potato masher until it thickens to a desired consistency.

Per Serving: Calories: 330; Protein: 18g; Fat: 9g; Saturated Fat: 2.5g; Carbohydrates: 46g; Sugar: 2g; Sodium: 96mg; Fiber: 16g

SPICY CHORIZO, WHITE BEAN, AND KALE SOUP

45 MINUTES OR LESS, DAIRY-FREE, FREEZER-FRIENDLY, GLUTEN-FREE

Mexican chorizo, a spicy ground meat sausage, gives this soup a big flavor boost. If you can't find Mexican chorizo, don't substitute dry, cured Spanish chorizo—try hot Italian sausage instead. Using canned beans makes this a fast-cooking soup perfect for busy evenings, lazy weekends, or any time you might be craving a bowl of warm, spicy, comforting soup.

SERVES: 4

PREP TIME: 5 MINUTES

SAUTÉ TIME: 10 MINUTES

PRESSURIZATION TIME: 5 MINUTES

COOK TIME: 5 MINUTES ON "MANUAL" MODE UNDER HIGH PRESSURE

RELEASE: NATURAL RELEASE FOR 5 MINUTES, THEN QUICK RELEASE

TOTAL TIME: 30 MINUTES

1 tablespoon olive oil

8 ounces Mexican chorizo sausage, casings removed

1 onion, diced

2 garlic cloves, minced

4 cups Chicken Broth (page 16) or store-bought unsalted chicken broth

1 (15-ounce) can no-salt-added diced tomatoes

2 (15-ounce) cans low-sodium great northern beans, rinsed and drained

2 cups lacinato kale, trimmed and chopped

Salt

Freshly ground black pepper

1. Turn on the electric pressure cooker and select the "Sauté" mode. Heat the olive oil and cook the sausage, breaking up large pieces into small crumbles, for 3 minutes, or until browned. Retain about 1 tablespoon of fat in the pot. Transfer the chorizo to a plate lined with paper towels and set aside.

2. Cook the onion and garlic for 2 minutes, or until the onion is soft. Turn off the "Sauté" mode.

3. Add the broth, diced tomatoes with their juices, and beans, and stir to combine.

4. Secure the lid. Select the "Manual" mode, and set the cooking time for 5 minutes under High Pressure. When the cooking cycle is complete, natural release for 5 minutes, then quick release any remaining steam.

5. Select the "Sauté" mode again and bring the soup to a simmer. Stir in the chorizo and kale and cook for 5 minutes, or until the kale is wilted. Season with salt and pepper to taste.

TIP: When using lacinato kale (also called dinosaur or Tuscan kale) or other hearty greens, remove their tough stems and ribs before you chop them.

Per Serving: Calories: 494; Protein: 28g; Fat: 15g; Saturated Fat: 5g; Carbohydrates: 63g; Sugar: 9g; Sodium: 910mg; Fiber: 14g

SPICED CHICKPEA SOUP

It's no secret that we love foods with bold flavors in my house. This easy, nutritious vegan dish is inspired by the spices widely used in Indian cuisine and is a total flavor explosion that will impress your taste buds. If you're not a fan of Swiss chard, feel free to customize this soup with whichever vegetable you prefer—cauliflower florets or green peas would be great substitutes.

SERVES: 4

PREP TIME: 5 MINUTES

SAUTÉ TIME: 8 MINUTES

PRESSURIZATION TIME: 5 MINUTES

COOK TIME: 8 MINUTES ON "MANUAL" MODE UNDER HIGH PRESSURE

RELEASE: NATURAL RELEASE FOR 10 MINUTES, THEN QUICK RELEASE

TOTAL TIME: 36 MINUTES

2 tablespoons olive oil

1 onion, diced

4 garlic cloves, minced

1 tablespoon freshly grated ginger

1 teaspoon garam masala

1 teaspoon ground turmeric

½ teaspoon ground cumin

2 teaspoons paprika

½ teaspoon red pepper flakes

2 (15-ounce) cans chickpeas, rinsed and drained

2 cups Vegetable Broth (page 14) or store-bought unsalted vegetable broth

1½ cups coconut milk

3 cups Swiss chard, chopped

Salt

Freshly ground black pepper

Naan or pita, for serving

1. Turn on the electric pressure cooker and select the "Sauté" mode. Heat the olive oil and cook the onion for 2 minutes, or until soft. Add the garlic, ginger, garam masala, turmeric, cumin, paprika, and red pepper flakes and cook for 1 minute or until the spices are fragrant. Turn off the "Sauté" mode.

2. Add the chickpeas and broth, and stir to combine.

3. Secure the lid. Select the "Manual" mode, and set the cooking time for 8 minutes under High Pressure. When the cooking cycle is complete, natural release for 10 minutes, then quick release any remaining steam.

4. Select the "Sauté" mode again and bring the soup to a simmer. Stir in the coconut milk and Swiss chard and cook for 5 minutes, or until the chard is wilted. Season with salt and pepper to taste. Serve with naan or pita.

TIP: Garam masala is an Indian spice blend that typically includes a mix of cumin, coriander, cardamom, black pepper, cinnamon, nutmeg, cloves, and fennel. The flavor is quite complex and intense. If you don't have any garam masala on hand, curry powder can be substituted in a pinch. It will change the flavor quite a bit, but it will still be delicious!

Per Serving (without bread): Calories: 441; Protein: 12g; Fat: 28g; Saturated Fat: 17g; Carbohydrates: 39g; Sugar: 7.5g; Sodium: 364mg; Fiber: 11g

MEXICAN-INSPIRED CHARRO BEAN SOUP

DAIRY-FREE, FREEZER-FRIENDLY

Having lived in South Texas for several years, my family and I have enjoyed our fair share of Tex-Mex food. Charro bean soup (sometimes called *borracho* beans) is one of the dishes I miss most. It's an essential side dish usually served in a Styrofoam cup alongside street tacos or to round out a meaty barbecue feast. This is my take on the bean soup from our favorite barbecue joint, but it packs some spicy heat! If you like yours mild, substitute an Anaheim or poblano pepper for the jalapeño and use ½ teaspoon of adobo sauce instead of the chipotle pepper itself.

SERVES: 6

PREP TIME: 5 MINUTES

SAUTÉ TIME: 7 MINUTES

PRESSURIZATION TIME: 10 MINUTES

COOK TIME: 20 MINUTES ON "MANUAL" MODE UNDER HIGH PRESSURE

RELEASE: NATURAL RELEASE FOR 15 MINUTES, THEN QUICK RELEASE

TOTAL TIME: 57 MINUTES

6 bacon slices, diced

1 onion, diced

3 garlic cloves, minced

2 jalapeño peppers, seeded and diced

1 small chipotle pepper in adobo sauce, minced

1 teaspoon dried oregano

½ teaspoon ground cumin

2 bay leaves

1 pound dried pinto beans, soaked overnight, rinsed, and drained

2 (10-ounce) cans diced tomatoes with green chiles

2 cups Chicken Broth (page 16) or store-bought unsalted chicken broth

1 (12-ounce) bottle Mexican-style beer

Salt

Freshly ground black pepper

1. Turn on the electric pressure cooker and select the "Sauté" mode. Cook the bacon for 5 minutes, or until crisp. Retain about 1 tablespoon of bacon fat in the pot. Transfer the bacon to a plate lined with paper towels and set aside.

2. Add the onion, garlic, and jalapeño peppers and cook for 2 minutes, or until the vegetables are soft. Turn off the "Sauté" mode. Add the bacon, chipotle pepper, oregano, cumin, bay leaves, beans, diced tomatoes with green chiles and their juices, broth, and beer, and stir to combine.

3. Secure the lid. Select the "Manual" mode, and set the cooking time for 20 minutes under High Pressure. When the cooking cycle is complete, natural release for 15 minutes, then quick release any remaining steam.

4. Remove and discard the bay leaves.

5. Using an immersion blender, traditional blender, or food processor, partially blend the soup for a thicker consistency if desired. Season with salt and pepper to taste.

TIP: My favorite beer to use in this recipe is Negra Modelo, but any Mexican-style lager or pilsner should work. Some people contend that pressure cooking doesn't cook off the alcohol. If you are worried about residual alcohol in the soup, just select "Sauté" mode after releasing the pressure and simmer it for 5 minutes uncovered, or simply substitute chicken broth for the beer if you'd like.

Per Serving: Calories: 362; Protein: 21g; Fat: 6g; Saturated Fat: 2g; Carbohydrates: 53g; Sugar: 3.5g; Sodium: 583mg; Fiber: 17g

MINESTRONE SOUP

Minestrone is a versatile dish that uses whatever ingredients you have. This version is loaded with onion, carrots, celery, zucchini, tomatoes, red kidney beans, and baby spinach for a simple and satisfying meal that totally hits the spot and tastes great with a sprinkle of Parmesan. I also love that this recipe requires hardly any hands-on cooking time, which is the kind of dinner I'd like to make after coming home from a busy day at work.

SERVES: 6

PREP TIME: 5 MINUTES

SAUTÉ TIME: 1 MINUTE

PRESSURIZATION TIME: 10 MINUTES

COOK TIME: 6 MINUTES ON "MANUAL" MODE UNDER HIGH PRESSURE

RELEASE: QUICK RELEASE

TOTAL TIME: 22 MINUTES

1 onion, diced

3 garlic cloves, minced

2 carrots, peeled and diced

2 celery stalks, diced

1 zucchini, diced

1 teaspoon dried basil

1 teaspoon dried oregano

1 bay leaf

1 (28-ounce) can crushed tomatoes

1 (15-ounce) can red kidney beans, rinsed and drained

4 cups Vegetable Broth (page 14) or store-bought unsalted vegetable broth

1 Parmesan rind (optional)

2 cups fresh baby spinach

Salt

Freshly ground black pepper

Grated Parmesan, for serving

1. Place the onion, garlic, carrots, celery, zucchini, basil, oregano, bay leaf, crushed tomatoes, beans, broth, and Parmesan rind (if using) into the inner pot of the pressure cooker, and stir to combine.

2. Secure the lid. Select the "Manual" mode, and set the cooking time for 6 minutes under High Pressure. When the cooking cycle is complete, quick release any remaining steam.

3. Remove and discard the bay leaf and Parmesan rind.

4. Select the "Sauté" mode and bring the soup to a simmer. Then, stir in the baby spinach and cook for 1 minute, or until wilted. Turn the electric pressure cooker off.

5. Season with salt and pepper to taste, sprinkle with Parmesan, and serve.

TIP: As a vegan option, leave out the Parmesan rind and the grated Parmesan.

Per Serving (without garnish): Calories: 157; Protein: 9g; Fat: 0.5g; Saturated Fat: 0g; Carbohydrates: 30g; Sugar: 8.5g; Sodium: 433mg; Fiber: 9g

MEDITERRANEAN-STYLE LENTIL SOUP

I love cooking with lentils because they're so versatile and soak up the flavors of the cooking liquid like a sponge. Lentils don't need to be soaked before cooking, which means you can make a pot of this soup any time you need a healthy, nourishing meal. One bowl will fill you up, and leftovers are perfect to freeze for future meals. Whether you're vegan, vegetarian, or just trying to incorporate more meatless protein into your diet, this is a soup you'll want to add to your dinner rotation.

SERVES: 6

PREP TIME: 5 MINUTES

SAUTÉ TIME: 2 MINUTES

PRESSURIZATION TIME: 10 MINUTES

COOK TIME: 15 MINUTES ON "MANUAL" MODE UNDER HIGH PRESSURE

RELEASE: NATURAL RELEASE FOR 15 MINUTES, THEN QUICK RELEASE

TOTAL TIME: 47 MINUTES

2 tablespoons olive oil

1 onion, diced

4 garlic cloves, minced

2 carrots, peeled and diced

2 celery stalks, diced

1 teaspoon smoked paprika

1 teaspoon ground cumin

1 teaspoon ground coriander

1½ cups dried green lentils, rinsed and drained

1 (15-ounce) can diced fire-roasted tomatoes

1 (15-ounce) can crushed tomatoes

4 cups Vegetable Broth (page 14) or store-bought unsalted vegetable broth

Salt

Freshly ground black pepper

1. Turn on the electric pressure cooker and select the "Sauté" mode. Heat the olive oil and cook the onion and garlic for 2 minutes, or until the onion is soft. Turn off the "Sauté" mode.

2. Add the carrots, celery, paprika, cumin, coriander, lentils, diced tomatoes with their juices, crushed tomatoes, and broth, and stir to combine.

3. Secure the lid. Select the "Manual" mode, and set the cooking time for 15 minutes under High Pressure. When the cooking cycle is complete, natural release for 15 minutes, then quick release any remaining steam.

4. Season with salt and pepper to taste.

TIP: When using dried lentils, it's important to rinse and sort the lentils well to ensure that there are no rocks or debris.

Per Serving: Calories: 284; Protein: 15g; Fat: 5g; Saturated Fat: 0.5g; Carbohydrates: 46g; Sugar: 8.5g; Sodium: 332mg; Fiber: 9g

MOROCCAN-INSPIRED HARIRA SOUP

45 MINUTES OR LESS, DAIRY-FREE, FREEZER-FRIENDLY, GLUTEN-FREE

Harira is a spiced Moroccan-inspired soup served year-round, but most commonly eaten during the fasting month of Ramadan. Although this version includes meat, vegetables, lentils, and chickpeas for a more substantial soup, you can omit the meat and substitute vegetable broth to turn it into a vegan dish. It will keep for a few days in the refrigerator and tastes even better the next day, as the flavors have had time to mingle and deepen. Simply reheat the soup and garnish it with freshly chopped cilantro and parsley.

SERVES: 6

PREP TIME: 5 MINUTES

SAUTÉ TIME: 7 MINUTES

PRESSURIZATION TIME: 10 MINUTES

COOK TIME: 15 MINUTES ON "MANUAL" MODE UNDER HIGH PRESSURE

RELEASE: QUICK RELEASE

TOTAL TIME: 37 MINUTES

1 tablespoon olive oil

8 ounces ground lamb or beef

1 onion, diced

4 garlic cloves, minced

1 carrot, diced

1 celery stalk, diced

½ teaspoon turmeric

¼ teaspoon paprika

½ teaspoon ground cumin

1 teaspoon harissa paste

Pinch ground cinnamon

⅓ cup dried green lentils, rinsed and drained

1 (15-ounce) can chickpeas, rinsed and drained

1 (15-ounce) can crushed tomatoes

3 cups Chicken Broth (page 16) or store-bought unsalted chicken broth

Salt

Freshly ground black pepper

1. Turn on the electric pressure cooker and select the "Sauté" mode. Heat the olive oil and cook the ground lamb for 5 minutes, or until browned. Drain off excess grease, leaving about 1 tablespoon of oil in the pot.

2. Add the onion and garlic and cook for 2 minutes, or until the onion is soft. Turn off the "Sauté" mode.

3. Add the carrot, celery, turmeric, paprika, cumin, harissa paste, cinnamon, lentils, chickpeas, crushed tomatoes, and broth, and stir to combine.

4. Secure the lid. Select the "Manual" mode, and set the cooking time for 15 minutes under High Pressure. When the cooking cycle is complete, quick release any remaining steam.

5. Season with salt and pepper to taste.

TIP: Harissa paste is a North African condiment made with simple ingredients like dried chiles, garlic, oil, vinegar, and spices. It can usually be found in the spice aisle of any supermarket, but if it's not available, sriracha or red pepper flakes will work as a substitute.

Per Serving: Calories: 231; Protein: 13g; Fat: 9g; Saturated Fat: 2.5g; Carbohydrates: 24g; Sugar: 5.5g; Sodium: 327mg; Fiber: 6g

PASTA E FAGIOLI

45 MINUTES OR LESS, DAIRY-FREE

Pasta e Fagioli is a traditional Italian soup that is made with vegetables and often has some beans and pasta in the mix. And if a cozy bowl of soup isn't enough, you can serve it with some garlic bread to dip in and soak up the last glorious drop. This is a great recipe to have in your repertoire for when you need a quick meal, and you can add some Parmesan on top as a garnish if you like.

SERVES: 6

PREP TIME: 5 MINUTES

SAUTÉ TIME: 7 MINUTES

PRESSURIZATION TIME: 10 MINUTES

COOK TIME: 4 MINUTES ON "MANUAL" MODE UNDER HIGH PRESSURE

RELEASE: QUICK RELEASE

TOTAL TIME: 26 MINUTES

1 tablespoon olive oil

1 pound mild or spicy Italian sausage, casings removed

1 small onion, diced

3 garlic cloves, minced

2 celery stalks, diced

2 carrots, peeled and diced

1½ teaspoons Italian seasoning

2 bay leaves

⅔ cup ditalini or any small pasta

1 (15-ounce) can no-salt-added diced tomatoes

1 (15-ounce) can no-salt-added tomato sauce

1 (15-ounce) can low-sodium great northern beans, rinsed and drained

1 (15-ounce) can low-sodium red kidney beans, rinsed and drained

4 cups Chicken Broth (page 16) or store-bought unsalted chicken broth or water

Salt

Freshly ground black pepper

1. Turn on the electric pressure cooker and select the "Sauté" mode. Heat the olive oil and cook the sausage, breaking up the large pieces into small crumbles, for 5 minutes, or until browned. Add the onion and garlic and cook for 2 minutes, or until the onion is soft. Turn off the "Sauté" mode.

2. Add the celery, carrots, Italian seasoning, bay leaves, ditalini, diced tomatoes with their juices, tomato sauce, beans, and broth, and stir to combine.

3. Secure the lid. Select the "Manual" mode, and set the cooking time for 4 minutes under High Pressure. When the cooking cycle is complete, quick release any remaining steam.

4. Remove and discard the bay leaves.

5. Season with salt and pepper to taste.

TIP: Whenever you make soup with pasta, consider cooking the pasta separately and stirring it into the soup just before serving. That way, the pasta won't become overcooked and mushy. Keeping the pasta separate is an especially good idea if you expect to have leftovers.

Per Serving: Calories: 521; Protein: 26g; Fat: 25g; Saturated Fat: 9g; Carbohydrates: 50g; Sugar: 11g; Sodium: 927mg; Fiber: 11g

NEPALI-STYLE CURRIED LENTIL SOUP

45 MINUTES OR LESS, DAIRY-FREE, FREEZER-FRIENDLY, GLUTEN-FREE, VEGAN

The first time my husband and I had Nepali *dal bhat* (curried lentils with rice), it was after a long, strenuous day of trekking in the Himalayas. Often served with pickled vegetables, chutney, basmati rice, and pappadum, it made for a well-balanced dish that we looked forward to eating every day for energy with as many helpings as we needed to conquer those high peaks. Every cook has their own recipe, but we've never tasted a *dal* we didn't like, so I decided to take inspiration from the flavors of the warm spices and aromatics and adapt them into a soup. I hope you love it as much as we do.

SERVES: 6

PREP TIME: 5 MINUTES

SAUTÉ TIME: 3 MINUTES

PRESSURIZATION TIME: 12 MINUTES

COOK TIME: 10 MINUTES ON "MANUAL" MODE UNDER HIGH PRESSURE

RELEASE: NATURAL RELEASE FOR 15 MINUTES, THEN QUICK RELEASE

TOTAL TIME: 45 MINUTES

2 tablespoons vegetable oil

1 onion, diced

3 garlic cloves, minced

1 tablespoon freshly grated ginger

1 teaspoon garam masala

½ teaspoon ground turmeric

1 teaspoon ground cumin

1 teaspoon ground coriander

1½ cups dried red lentils, rinsed and drained

6 cups Vegetable Broth (page 14) or store-bought unsalted vegetable broth

Salt

Freshly ground black pepper

1. Turn on the electric pressure cooker and select the "Sauté" mode. Heat the vegetable oil and cook the onion and garlic for 2 minutes, or until the onion is soft. Add the ginger, garam masala, turmeric, cumin, and coriander and cook for 1 minute or until the spices are fragrant. Turn off the "Sauté" mode.

2. Add the lentils and broth, and stir to combine.

3. Secure the lid. Select the "Manual" mode, and set the cooking time for 10 minutes under High Pressure. When the cooking cycle is complete, natural release for 15 minutes, then quick release any remaining steam.

4. Season with salt and pepper to taste.

TIP: Red or yellow lentils are best for this recipe. Brown or green lentils also taste great, but take longer to cook. If you're using these, just increase the cooking time to 15 minutes under High Pressure.

Per Serving: Calories: 241; Protein: 13g; Fat: 5.5g; Saturated Fat: 1g; Carbohydrates: 36g; Sugar: 2.5g; Sodium: 28mg; Fiber: 6.5g

TUSCAN-STYLE WHITE BEAN SOUP WITH PANCETTA AND ROSEMARY (RIBOLLITA)

Ribollita is Italian for "reboiled," which describes how this soup was originally made: by repurposing leftover vegetable soups from the previous day. This thick, hearty soup is popular throughout Tuscany, and there are as many variations as there are cooks. It always includes stale bread to help thicken the soup, and this version calls for savory pancetta and woodsy rosemary, both of which add tons of robust flavor to this rustic dish.

SERVES: 6

PREP TIME: 5 MINUTES

SAUTÉ TIME: 7 MINUTES

PRESSURIZATION TIME:
10 MINUTES

COOK TIME: 5 MINUTES ON "MANUAL" MODE UNDER HIGH PRESSURE

RELEASE: NATURAL RELEASE FOR 10 MINUTES, THEN QUICK RELEASE

TOTAL TIME: 37 MINUTES

4 ounces pancetta, diced

1 small onion, diced

2 garlic cloves, minced

1 carrot, peeled and diced

1 celery stalk, diced

2 rosemary sprigs

¼ teaspoon red pepper flakes

1 bay leaf

1 tablespoon tomato paste

2 (15-ounce) cans cannellini beans, rinsed and drained

3 slices day-old rustic bread, torn into small pieces

4 cups lacinato kale or green cabbage, trimmed and chopped

4 cups Chicken Broth (page 16) or Vegetable Broth (page 14) or store-bought unsalted chicken or vegetable broth

Salt

Freshly ground black pepper

Extra-virgin olive oil, for serving

Grated Parmesan, for serving

continued >

TUSCAN-STYLE WHITE BEAN SOUP WITH PANCETTA AND ROSEMARY (RIBOLLITA)

continued

1. Turn on the electric pressure cooker and select the "Sauté" mode. Cook the pancetta for 5 minutes, or until crisp. Retain about 1 tablespoon of fat in the pot. Transfer the pancetta to a plate lined with paper towels and set aside.

2. Add the onion and garlic and cook for 2 minutes, or until the onion is soft. Turn off the "Sauté" mode.

3. Add the pancetta, carrot, celery, rosemary, red pepper flakes, bay leaf, tomato paste, beans, bread, kale, and broth, and stir to combine.

4. Secure the lid. Select the "Manual" mode, and set the cooking time for 5 minutes under High Pressure. When the cooking cycle is complete, natural release for 10 minutes, then quick release any remaining steam.

5. Remove and discard the rosemary sprigs and bay leaf.

6. Season with salt and pepper to taste. Serve drizzled with olive oil and sprinkled with grated Parmesan.

TIP: Pancetta is pork belly cured with salt, black pepper, and spices and rolled into a cylinder. Replacing pancetta with bacon works just as well in this recipe.

Per Serving (without garnish): Calories: 266; Protein: 16g; Fat: 7.5g; Saturated Fat: 2.5g; Carbohydrates: 31g; Sugar: 3.5g; Sodium: 764mg; Fiber: 5.5g

SWEET POTATO, BLACK BEAN, AND QUINOA CHILI

45 MINUTES OR LESS, DAIRY-FREE, FREEZER-FRIENDLY, GLUTEN-FREE, VEGAN

Made with quinoa, sweet potatoes, and black beans, this vegan chili comes together quickly without sacrificing the rich flavors all chilis should have. It's wholesome, filling, and has just the right amount of spiciness to satisfy everyone. Cut back on the chili powder if you don't like things too spicy or add a jalapeño pepper or more chipotle peppers if you like things extra spicy. Then, serve it with your preferred combination of sour cream, sliced scallions, sliced avocado, and tortilla chips.

SERVES: 6

PREP TIME: 5 MINUTES

SAUTÉ TIME: 2 MINUTES

PRESSURIZATION TIME:
5 MINUTES

COOK TIME: 8 MINUTES ON "MANUAL" MODE UNDER HIGH PRESSURE

RELEASE: QUICK RELEASE

TOTAL TIME: 20 MINUTES

1 tablespoon olive oil

1 onion, diced

3 garlic cloves, minced

2 sweet potatoes, peeled and cubed

1 small red bell pepper, seeded and diced

1 cup fresh or frozen corn kernels

1 tablespoon chili powder

½ teaspoon dried oregano

1 teaspoon ground cumin

1 chipotle pepper in adobo sauce, minced

1 (28-ounce) can diced fire-roasted tomatoes

1 (15-ounce) can black beans, rinsed and drained

½ cup uncooked quinoa, rinsed and drained

2½ cups Vegetable Broth (page 14) or store-bought unsalted vegetable broth

Salt

Freshly ground black pepper

continued >

SWEET POTATO, BLACK BEAN, AND QUINOA CHILI

continued

1. Turn on the electric pressure cooker and select the "Sauté" mode. Heat the olive oil and cook the onion and garlic for 2 minutes, or until the onion is soft. Turn off the "Sauté" mode.

2. Add the sweet potatoes, bell pepper, corn, chili powder, oregano, cumin, chipotle pepper, diced tomatoes with their juices, beans, quinoa, and broth, and stir to combine.

3. Secure the lid. Select the "Manual" mode, and set the cooking time for 8 minutes under High Pressure. When the cooking cycle is complete, quick release any remaining steam.

4. Season with salt and pepper to taste.

TIP: Use the leftovers of this chili as a meatless topping on nachos, cheese fries, or vegetarian hot dogs.

Per Serving: Calories: 249; Protein: 10g; Fat: 4g; Saturated Fat: 0.5g; Carbohydrates: 45g; Sugar: 10g; Sodium: 459mg; Fiber: 9g

CAJUN-STYLE 16-BEAN SOUP WITH ANDOUILLE SAUSAGE

DAIRY-FREE, FREEZER-FRIENDLY, GLUTEN-FREE

Beans are a nutrition powerhouse, and when you've got 16 different varieties all in one pot, you reap the benefits of every type. I love how beautiful this soup is; each bite is different with all sorts of colors, patterns, and sizes. Fifteen- or 16-bean mixes can be found in the dried bean section of most major grocery stores, but feel free to create your own mix with whatever leftover beans you have.

SERVES: 6

PREP TIME: 5 MINUTES

SAUTÉ TIME: 7 MINUTES

PRESSURIZATION TIME:
10 MINUTES

COOK TIME: 20 MINUTES ON "MANUAL" MODE UNDER HIGH PRESSURE

RELEASE: NATURAL RELEASE FOR 15 MINUTES, THEN QUICK RELEASE

TOTAL TIME: 57 MINUTES

1 tablespoon olive oil

1 pound smoked andouille sausage, sliced

1 onion, diced

1 green bell pepper, seeded and diced

2 celery stalks, diced

1 pound 16-bean soup mix, soaked overnight, rinsed, and drained

2 teaspoons salt-free Cajun seasoning

1 (8-ounce) can tomato sauce

5 cups Chicken Broth (page 16) or store-bought unsalted chicken broth

Salt

Freshly ground black pepper

continued >

CAJUN-STYLE 16-BEAN SOUP WITH ANDOUILLE SAUSAGE

continued

1. Turn on the electric pressure cooker and select the "Sauté" mode. Heat the olive oil and cook the sausage for 3 minutes, or until browned on both sides. Add the onion, bell pepper, and celery and cook for 4 minutes, or until the vegetables are soft. Turn off the "Sauté" mode.

2. Add the beans, Cajun seasoning, tomato sauce, and broth, and stir to combine.

3. Secure the lid. Select the "Manual" mode, and set the cooking time for 20 minutes under High Pressure. When the cooking cycle is complete, natural release for 15 minutes, then quick release any remaining steam.

4. Season with salt and pepper to taste.

TIP: Most bean soup mixes found in major grocery stores come with a seasoning packet, which I usually reserve for another use (I don't recommend using it for this recipe since the blend may contain salt and ham or poultry flavoring, which makes it difficult to adjust the seasoning given the salt from the andouille sausage). To make your own Cajun seasoning blend, combine 1 tablespoon of paprika, 2 teaspoons of garlic powder, 1 teaspoon of onion powder, 1 teaspoon of freshly ground black pepper, 1 teaspoon of white pepper, 1 teaspoon of dried oregano, ½ teaspoon of dried thyme, and ½ teaspoon of cayenne pepper until they're evenly blended.

Per Serving: Calories: 421; Protein: 30g; Fat: 13g; Saturated Fat: 4g; Carbohydrates: 47g; Sugar: 7g; Sodium: 948mg; Fiber: 12g

SPLIT PEA SOUP

This classic soup makes for a nutritious, filling, and inexpensive meal that's perfect for cold nights. You don't have to soak the split peas, which means it's great for days when you're too busy to plan your meals in advance. The soup is delicious on its own, but if you have time, be sure to make some brown butter croutons to serve with it (see recipe tip); the nutty, crunchy bites are an amazing match for this creamy soup.

SERVES: 6

PREP TIME: 5 MINUTES

PRESSURIZATION TIME: 12 MINUTES

COOK TIME: 15 MINUTES ON "MANUAL" MODE UNDER HIGH PRESSURE

RELEASE: NATURAL RELEASE FOR 10 MINUTES, THEN QUICK RELEASE

TOTAL TIME: 42 MINUTES

1 onion, diced

3 garlic cloves, minced

2 carrots, peeled and diced

2 celery stalks, diced

¼ teaspoon dried thyme

1 bay leaf

1 pound green split peas, rinsed and drained

1 pound smoked ham hock or smoked turkey wing

6 cups Chicken Broth (page 16) or store-bought unsalted chicken broth

Salt

Freshly ground black pepper

continued >

SPLIT PEA SOUP

continued

1. Place the onion, garlic, carrots, celery, thyme, bay leaf, split peas, ham hock, and broth in the inner pot of the pressure cooker, and stir to combine.

2. Secure the lid. Select the "Manual" mode, and set the cooking time for 15 minutes under High Pressure. When the cooking cycle is complete, natural release for 10 minutes, then quick release any remaining steam.

3. Remove and discard the bay leaf and ham hock.

4. Season with salt and pepper to taste.

TIP: Brown butter croutons are a delicious addition to this soup. To make them, melt 3 tablespoons of unsalted butter in a small saucepan and simmer over medium heat for 3 minutes, or until the butter becomes golden brown and aromatic. In a large baking sheet, toss the brown butter with 3 cups of sourdough bread cubes and season with salt and freshly ground pepper to taste. Bake at 350°F for 10 to 15 minutes, or until toasted and golden brown, stirring occasionally. Remove the croutons from oven and let them cool completely on the baking sheet before serving.

Per Serving: Calories: 319; Protein: 21g; Fat: 6.5g; Saturated Fat: 2g; Carbohydrates: 46g; Sugar: 8.5g; Sodium: 247mg; Fiber: 17g

BLACK-EYED PEA, HAM BONE, AND COLLARD GREENS SOUP

DAIRY-FREE, FREEZER-FRIENDLY, GLUTEN-FREE

Eating black-eyed peas and greens on New Year's Day is a time-honored tradition in the South for good luck and prosperity in the new year. You'll love the creamy, melt-in-your-mouth texture from the black-eyed peas, with the collard greens providing more texture and substance. Put a leftover meaty ham bone to good use and enjoy this soup any day of the year for a satisfying, warming meal.

SERVES: 6

PREP TIME: 5 MINUTES

SAUTÉ TIME: 2 MINUTES

PRESSURIZATION TIME: 12 MINUTES

COOK TIME: 20 MINUTES ON "MANUAL" MODE UNDER HIGH PRESSURE

RELEASE: NATURAL RELEASE FOR 15 MINUTES, THEN QUICK RELEASE

TOTAL TIME: 54 MINUTES

2 tablespoons olive oil

1 onion, diced

3 garlic cloves, minced

1 carrot, peeled and diced

1 celery stalk, diced

1 teaspoon smoked paprika

1 bay leaf

1 pound dried black-eyed peas, rinsed and drained

1 leftover ham bone or 2 cups diced ham

2 cups collard greens, tough stems and ribs removed and finely chopped

6 cups Chicken Broth (page 16) or store-bought unsalted chicken broth

Salt

Freshly ground black pepper

continued >

BLACK-EYED PEA, HAM BONE, AND COLLARD GREENS SOUP

continued

1. Turn on the electric pressure cooker and select the "Sauté" mode. Heat the olive oil and cook the onion and garlic for 2 minutes, or until the onion is soft. Turn off the "Sauté" mode.

2. Add the carrot, celery, paprika, bay leaf, black-eyed peas, ham bone, collard greens, and broth, and stir to combine.

3. Secure the lid. Select the "Manual" mode, and set the cooking time for 20 minutes under High Pressure. When the cooking cycle is complete, natural release for 15 minutes, then quick release any remaining steam.

4. Remove and discard the bay leaf. Remove the ham bone, chop up the meat into smaller pieces, and add it to the soup.

5. Season with salt and pepper to taste.

TIP: Chard (Swiss or rainbow) or mustard greens can be used in place of the collard greens.

Per Serving: Calories: 373; Protein: 28g; Fat: 7.5g; Saturated Fat: 1.5g; Carbohydrates: 50g; Sugar: 9.5g; Sodium: 620mg; Fiber: 15g

BUTTER BEAN SOUP WITH CABBAGE AND HAM

DAIRY-FREE, FREEZER-FRIENDLY, GLUTEN-FREE

This recipe is all about going back to the basics; it requires just a few simple ingredients, yet the whole is greater than the sum of its parts. Creamy butter beans (often sold as large lima beans) have a velvety texture and rich, savory, almost buttery flavor.

SERVES: 6

PREP TIME: 5 MINUTES

PRESSURIZATION TIME: 16 MINUTES

COOK TIME: 20 MINUTES ON "MANUAL" MODE UNDER HIGH PRESSURE

RELEASE: NATURAL RELEASE FOR 10 MINUTES, THEN QUICK RELEASE

TOTAL TIME: 51 MINUTES

1 onion, diced

2 garlic cloves, minced

1 rosemary sprig

1 pound dried butter beans or lima beans, soaked overnight, rinsed, and drained

2 cups diced ham

2 cups chopped green cabbage

1 teaspoon red wine vinegar

7 cups Chicken Broth (page 16) or store-bought unsalted chicken broth

Salt

Freshly ground black pepper

1. Place the onion, garlic, rosemary, beans, ham, cabbage, vinegar, and broth in the inner pot of the pressure cooker, and stir to combine.

2. Secure the lid. Select the "Manual" mode, and set the cooking time for 20 minutes under High Pressure. When the cooking cycle is complete, natural release for 10 minutes, then quick release any remaining steam.

3. Season with salt and pepper to taste.

TIP: Because this soup is so simple, it really needs a good-quality broth. If you're using store-bought broth, be sure to use a low-sodium variety since the diced ham will add salt to the soup.

Per Serving: Calories: 176; Protein: 17g; Fat: 2.5g; Saturated Fat: 1g; Carbohydrates: 22g; Sugar: 4.5g; Sodium: 630mg; Fiber: 5g

FARMERS' MARKET VEGETABLE AND FARRO SOUP

DAIRY-FREE, FREEZER-FRIENDLY

When I was living in New York City, I would head to the Union Square farmers' market on the weekend and buy the most enticing seasonal produce. This encouraged me to taste different vegetables and try new dishes when I got home. This soup was inspired by the farmers' market vegetables I could get my hands on, with the addition of farro, an Italian ancient whole grain that adds a slightly nutty flavor and a firm, chewy texture to this vegetable soup.

SERVES: 6

PREP TIME: 5 MINUTES

SAUTÉ TIME: 7 MINUTES

PRESSURIZATION TIME:
12 MINUTES

COOK TIME: 12 MINUTES ON "MANUAL" MODE UNDER HIGH PRESSURE

RELEASE: NATURAL RELEASE FOR 10 MINUTES, THEN QUICK RELEASE

TOTAL TIME: 46 MINUTES

1 tablespoon olive oil

1 onion, diced

2 garlic cloves, minced

1 carrot, peeled and diced

2 plum tomatoes, seeded and diced

2 cups fresh corn kernels

1 teaspoon Italian seasoning

2 bay leaves

1 tablespoon tomato paste

⅔ cup uncooked pearled farro, rinsed and drained

6 cups Chicken Broth (page 16) or Vegetable Broth (page 14) or store-bought unsalted chicken or vegetable broth

2 zucchini or yellow summer squash, diced

1 cup freshly cut green beans, cut into 1-inch pieces

Salt

Freshly ground black pepper

1. Turn on the electric pressure cooker and select the "Sauté" mode. Heat the olive oil and cook the onion and garlic for 2 minutes, or until the onion is soft. Turn off the "Sauté" mode.

2. Add the carrot, tomatoes, corn, Italian seasoning, bay leaves, tomato paste, farro, and broth, and stir to combine.

3. Secure the lid. Select the "Manual" mode, and set the cooking time for 12 minutes under High Pressure. When the cooking cycle is complete, natural release for 10 minutes, then quick release any remaining steam.

4. Select the "Sauté" mode again and bring the soup to a simmer. Then, stir in the zucchini and green beans and cook for 5 minutes, or until the vegetables are tender. Turn the electric pressure cooker off.

5. Season with salt and pepper to taste.

TIP: There are different kinds of farro available, such as whole grain, pearled, semi-pearled, and quick-cooking farro, which could take more or less time to cook. The cooking time in this recipe is for Italian pearled farro. If you are using another type, you'll need to adjust the cooking time accordingly.

Per Serving: Calories: 183; Protein: 9g; Fat: 3g; Saturated Fat: 0.5g; Carbohydrates: 33g; Sugar: 9g; Sodium: 235mg; Fiber: 4gg

MUSHROOM AND WILD RICE SOUP

GLUTEN-FREE

I'm a big fan of mushroom soups, and this one is no exception. While I make this soup at any time of the year, there's something that makes me crave it when the days grow shorter and the temperatures drop. Maybe it's the earthy umami flavor or the "meaty" texture of the mushrooms or the nutty, chewy wild rice. Either way, if you love mushrooms, you must try this recipe.

SERVES: 4

PREP TIME: 5 MINUTES

SAUTÉ TIME: 1 MINUTE

PRESSURIZATION TIME:
10 MINUTES

COOK TIME: 35 MINUTES ON "MANUAL" MODE UNDER HIGH PRESSURE

RELEASE: QUICK RELEASE

TOTAL TIME: 51 MINUTES

1 small onion, diced

3 garlic cloves, minced

2 carrots, peeled and diced

2 celery stalks, diced

3 thyme sprigs

1 pound mixed fresh mushrooms, sliced

1 cup wild rice, rinsed and drained

4 cups Chicken Broth (page 16) or Vegetable Broth (page 14) or store-bought unsalted version

¼ cup all-purpose flour

1 cup milk

Salt

Freshly ground black pepper

1. Place the onion, garlic, carrots, celery, thyme, mushrooms, wild rice, and broth in the inner pot of the pressure cooker, and stir to combine.

2. Secure the lid. Select the "Manual" mode, and set the cooking time for 35 minutes under High Pressure. When the cooking cycle is complete, quick release any remaining steam.

3. In a separate bowl, whisk together the flour and milk. Select the "Sauté" mode and bring the soup to a simmer. Then, add the flour mixture and stir for 1 minute, or until the soup has thickened. Turn the electric pressure cooker off.

4. Season with salt and pepper to taste.

TIP: Make sure you're using plain wild rice and not a wild rice blend in this soup. Some wild rice blends contain wild rice mixed with brown, white, and red rice, and the softer grains of rice in the blend will thicken the soup too much.

Per Serving: Calories: 280; Protein: 15g; Fat: 2.5g; Saturated Fat: 1.5g; Carbohydrates: 52g; Sugar: 9,5g; Sodium: 199mg; Fiber: 5g

CABBAGE ROLL SOUP

Stuffed cabbage rolls are a classic dish that can be time-consuming and tedious to prepare. This soup has all the flavors and ingredients of stuffed cabbage rolls in a deconstructed soup form, with ground beef, rice, and cabbage simmering in a rich tomato and beef broth—indulgence in a fraction of the time!

SERVES: 6

PREP TIME: 5 MINUTES

SAUTÉ TIME: 7 MINUTES

PRESSURIZATION TIME:
12 MINUTES

COOK TIME: 5 MINUTES ON "MANUAL" MODE UNDER HIGH PRESSURE

RELEASE: NATURAL RELEASE FOR 15 MINUTES, THEN QUICK RELEASE

TOTAL TIME: 44 MINUTES

1 tablespoon olive oil

1 pound ground beef

1 onion, diced

2 garlic cloves, minced

1 teaspoon smoked paprika

½ teaspoon dried oregano

1 bay leaf

1 tablespoon Worcestershire sauce

1 tablespoon tomato paste

1 (28-ounce) can tomato puree

⅔ cup uncooked long-grain white rice

6 cups Roasted Beef Bone Stock (page 19) or store-bought unsalted beef broth

6 cups coarsely chopped green cabbage

Salt

Freshly ground black pepper

continued >

CABBAGE ROLL SOUP

continued

1. Turn on the electric pressure cooker and select the "Sauté" mode. Heat the olive oil and cook the beef for 5 minutes, or until browned. Drain off excess grease, leaving about 1 tablespoon of oil in the pot.

2. Add the onion and garlic and cook for 2 minutes, or until the onion is soft. Turn off the "Sauté" mode.

3. Add the paprika, oregano, bay leaf, Worcestershire sauce, tomato paste, tomato puree, rice, stock, and cabbage, and stir to combine.

4. Secure the lid. Select the "Manual" mode, and set the cooking time for 5 minutes under High Pressure. When the cooking cycle is complete, natural release for 15 minutes, then quick release any remaining steam.

5. Season with salt and pepper to taste.

TIP: Leftovers will have a stew-like consistency as the rice sits and absorbs more of the broth. You can substitute brown rice for the white rice, which holds up better in leftovers; just change the cooking time to 20 minutes instead of 5 minutes.

Per Serving: Calories: 323; Protein: 20g; Fat: 11g; Saturated Fat: 4g; Carbohydrates: 36g; Sugar: 10g; Sodium: 431mg; Fiber: 5g

GRAINS AND GREENS SOUP

This simple grains and greens soup is brimming with wellness and is the type of soup I want to make when I'm in need of a serious healthy food fix. I add whatever grains and greens I have on hand and always add a leftover Parmesan rind before simmering for extra flavor. Sometimes, I'll serve it with grated Parmesan and a poached egg on top for additional protein and richness. Have some fun with this soup and truly make it your own.

SERVES: 6

PREP TIME: 5 MINUTES

SAUTÉ TIME: 2 MINUTES

PRESSURIZATION TIME:
12 MINUTES

COOK TIME: 25 MINUTES ON "MANUAL" MODE UNDER HIGH PRESSURE

RELEASE: QUICK RELEASE

TOTAL TIME: 44 MINUTES

1 tablespoon olive oil

1 small leek (white and light green parts only), thinly sliced

2 garlic cloves, minced

1 rosemary sprig

⅓ cup uncooked wheat berries, rinsed and drained

⅓ cup uncooked brown rice, rinsed and drained

6 cups Chicken Broth (page 16) or Vegetable Broth (page 14) or store-bought unsalted chicken or vegetable broth

4 cups escarole or Swiss chard, chopped

1 Parmesan rind (optional)

Salt

Freshly ground black pepper

continued >

GRAINS AND GREENS SOUP

continued

1. Turn on the electric pressure cooker and select the "Sauté" mode. Heat the olive oil and cook the leek and garlic for 2 minutes. Turn off the "Sauté" mode.

2. Add the rosemary, wheat berries, rice, broth, escarole, and Parmesan rind (if using), and stir to combine.

3. Secure the lid. Select the "Manual" mode, and set the cooking time for 25 minutes under High Pressure. When the cooking cycle is complete, quick release any remaining steam.

4. Remove and discard the rosemary sprig and Parmesan rind.

5. Season with salt and pepper to taste.

TIP: To make this soup gluten-free, substitute quinoa, millet, or additional brown rice for the wheat berries.

Per Serving: Calories: 123; Protein: 6g; Fat: 2.5g; Saturated Fat: 0.5g; Carbohydrates: 20g; Sugar: 1.5g; Sodium: 135mg; Fiber: 3g

HEARTY WINTER VEGETABLE AND BARLEY SOUP

Root vegetables can often be overlooked and underrated, but they definitely take the spotlight in this soup, which highlights the sweetness and earthiness of winter vegetables when paired with nutty-tasting barley. It is the meal I want to enjoy in front of a crackling fire when the first snow of the season falls. Even if you don't have snowy weather where you are, I promise this soup will hit the spot whenever you crave something heartwarming and comforting.

SERVES: 6

PREP TIME: 5 MINUTES

SAUTÉ TIME: 2 MINUTES

PRESSURIZATION TIME: 12 MINUTES

COOK TIME: 25 MINUTES ON "MANUAL" MODE UNDER HIGH PRESSURE

RELEASE: QUICK RELEASE

TOTAL TIME: 44 MINUTES

1 tablespoon olive oil

1 onion, diced

2 garlic cloves, minced

1 carrot, peeled and diced

1 parsnip, peeled and diced

1 rutabaga, peeled and diced

1 turnip, peeled and diced

2 bay leaves

2 thyme sprigs

1 cup uncooked pearled barley, rinsed and drained

6 cups Vegetable Broth (page 14) or store-bought unsalted vegetable broth

Salt

Freshly ground black pepper

Freshly chopped flat-leaf parsley, for garnish

continued >

HEARTY WINTER VEGETABLE AND BARLEY SOUP

continued

1. Turn on the electric pressure cooker and select the "Sauté" mode. Heat the olive oil and cook the onion and garlic for 2 minutes, or until the onion is soft. Turn off the "Sauté" mode.

2. Add the carrot, parsnip, rutabaga, turnip, bay leaves, thyme, barley, and broth, and stir to combine.

3. Secure the lid. Select the "Manual" mode, and set the cooking time for 25 minutes under High Pressure. When the cooking cycle is complete, quick release any remaining steam.

4. Remove and discard the bay leaves and thyme sprigs.

5. Season with salt and pepper to taste. Serve with the parsley.

TIP: Any mix of winter root vegetables can be used, although the greater variety, the better the soup will taste. Other options include sunchokes (Jerusalem artichokes), celeriac, acorn squash, and sweet potatoes.

Per Serving: Calories: 194; Protein: 5g; Fat: 3g; Saturated Fat: 0.5g; Carbohydrates: 39g; Sugar: 6g; Sodium: 49mg; Fiber: 8.5g

CHAPTER 5

POULTRY SOUPS

Perhaps the most comforting and nourishing soups are classic poultry recipes like Old-Fashioned Chicken Noodle Soup (page 88) and Italian-Style Wedding Soup with Turkey Meatballs (page 121). With the electric pressure cooker, you can create those same slow-cooked favorites in much less time.

Use these recipes as inspiration and feel free to change up the choice of meat (e.g., swapping thigh meat for breast meat or substituting turkey or duck for chicken). All of these soups make wonderful one-pot meals, perhaps served with a green salad and toasted bread on the side. If you're new to making soup, the recipes in this section are a great place to begin. You might even discover some new favorites!

< Chicken Pozole Verde, page 92

OLD-FASHIONED CHICKEN NOODLE SOUP

45 MINUTES OR LESS, DAIRY-FREE

While it's an absolute staple for cold winter days or flu season, I make this soup now and then, regardless of what the weather is like. Sometimes, there's no point in messing around with something simple and delicious. Everyone needs a trusty chicken noodle soup to pull out at a moment's notice, and I hope my recipe will become yours!

SERVES: 6

PREP TIME: 5 MINUTES

SAUTÉ TIME: 7 MINUTES

PRESSURIZATION TIME: 12 MINUTES

COOK TIME: 10 MINUTES ON "MANUAL" MODE UNDER HIGH PRESSURE

RELEASE: QUICK RELEASE

TOTAL TIME: 34 MINUTES

1 tablespoon unsalted butter

1 onion, diced

2 garlic cloves, minced

2 carrots, peeled and diced

2 celery stalks, diced

½ teaspoon dried thyme

1 bay leaf

1 pound boneless, skinless chicken breast

6 cups Chicken Broth (page 16) or store-bought unsalted chicken broth

2 cups uncooked egg noodles

Salt

Freshly ground black pepper

Freshly chopped flat-leaf parsley, for garnish

1. Turn on the electric pressure cooker and select the "Sauté" mode. Melt the butter and cook the onion and garlic for 2 minutes, or until the onion is soft. Turn off the "Sauté" mode.

2. Add the carrots, celery, thyme, bay leaf, chicken breast, and broth, and stir to combine.

3. Secure the lid. Select the "Manual" mode, and set the cooking time for 10 minutes under High Pressure. When the cooking cycle is complete, quick release any remaining steam.

4. Remove and discard the bay leaf.

5. Remove the chicken and shred it with two forks.

6. Select the "Sauté" mode again and bring the soup to a simmer. Then, stir in the egg noodles and cook for 5 minutes, or until tender. Stir in the shredded chicken and turn the electric pressure cooker off.

7. Season with salt and pepper to taste. Garnish with parsley before serving.

TIP: Substitute gluten-free egg noodles or pasta for a gluten-free version of this soup.

Per Serving: Calories: 214; Protein: 23g; Fat: 4.5g; Saturated Fat: 1.5g; Carbohydrates: 18g; Sugar: 3.5g; Sodium: 195mg; Fiber: 2g

LEMON CHICKEN ORZO SOUP

45 MINUTES OR LESS, DAIRY-FREE

If the goal is to pack as many flavors as possible into a bowl that still comes across as very light in flavor, I'd say this soup succeeds better than any other. It's made with such simple ingredients, yet it becomes something very complex and delicate. Orzo—a pasta shaped like a large grain of rice—is perfect for adding to soups, as it cooks much faster than most kinds of rice. Feeling under the weather and don't have much of an appetite? A bowl of this soup is the perfect fix.

SERVES: 6

PREP TIME: 5 MINUTES

SAUTÉ TIME: 12 MINUTES

PRESSURIZATION TIME: 12 MINUTES

COOK TIME: 10 MINUTES ON "MANUAL" MODE UNDER HIGH PRESSURE

RELEASE: QUICK RELEASE

TOTAL TIME: 39 MINUTES

2 tablespoons olive oil

1 onion, diced

3 garlic cloves, minced

2 carrots, peeled and diced

1 celery stalk, diced

1 rosemary sprig

1 teaspoon lemon zest

1 pound boneless, skinless chicken breast, cut into bite-size pieces

6 cups Chicken Broth (page 16) or store-bought unsalted chicken broth

1 cup uncooked orzo

2 tablespoons fresh lemon juice

3 cups baby spinach leaves

Salt

Freshly ground black pepper

1. Turn on the electric pressure cooker and select the "Sauté" mode. Heat the olive oil and cook the onion and garlic for 2 minutes, or until the onion is soft. Turn off the "Sauté" mode.

2. Add the carrots, celery, rosemary, lemon zest, chicken breast, and broth, and stir to combine.

3. Secure the lid. Select the "Manual" mode, and set the cooking time for 10 minutes under High Pressure. When the cooking cycle is complete, quick release any remaining steam.

4. Remove and discard the rosemary sprig.

5. Select the "Sauté" mode again and bring the soup to a simmer. Then, stir in the orzo and cook for 10 minutes, or until tender. Add the lemon juice and spinach, and stir until wilted. Turn the electric pressure cooker off.

6. Season with salt and pepper to taste.

TIP: If you can get them, Meyer lemons add a nice touch to this soup, giving it a softer lemon undertone with less acidity.

Per Serving: Calories: 270; Protein: 24g; Fat: 7g; Saturated Fat: 1g; Carbohydrates: 26g; Sugar: 4g; Sodium: 201mg; Fiber: 2.5g

CHICKEN POZOLE VERDE

This Mexican-inspired chicken soup gets its beautiful green hue from a salsa verde made with tangy tomatillos, spicy peppers, and fresh cilantro. Even though it has a stew-like consistency, it still tastes really refreshing and bright. The chewy texture and nutty flavor of hominy make it extra special and filling. If you want to add a little more heat and flavor, keep the seeds in the peppers.

SERVES: 6

PREP TIME: 5 MINUTES

SAUTÉ TIME: 4 MINUTES

PRESSURIZATION TIME:
10 MINUTES

COOK TIME: 20 MINUTES ON "MANUAL" MODE UNDER HIGH PRESSURE

RELEASE: QUICK RELEASE

TOTAL TIME: 39 MINUTES

---

1 onion, quartered

1 pound fresh tomatillos, coarsely chopped

1 poblano pepper, seeded and coarsely chopped

2 jalapeño peppers, seeded and coarsely chopped

½ cup packed cilantro

3 garlic cloves, smashed

4 cups Chicken Broth (page 16) or store-bought unsalted chicken broth, divided

2 tablespoons olive oil

1 pound boneless, skinless chicken breast or thighs

1 tablespoon dried oregano

1 teaspoon ground cumin

2 (15-ounce) cans hominy, rinsed and drained

Salt

Freshly ground black pepper

Thinly sliced radishes, for serving

Diced avocado, for serving

Crumbled cotija, for serving

Freshly chopped cilantro, for serving

Lime wedges, for serving

1. In a blender, place the onion, tomatillos, poblano pepper, jalapeño peppers, cilantro, garlic, and 2 cups of the broth and blend until smooth.

2. Turn on the electric pressure cooker and select the "Sauté" mode. Heat the olive oil and cook the chicken for 2 minutes per side, or until browned on both sides. Turn off the "Sauté" mode.

3. Add the tomatillo mixture, the remaining 2 cups broth, oregano, cumin, and hominy, and stir to combine.

4. Secure the lid. Select the "Manual" mode, and set the cooking time for 20 minutes under High Pressure. When the cooking cycle is complete, quick release any remaining steam.

5. Remove the chicken, shred it with two forks, and return it to the pot. Season the soup with salt and pepper to taste. Serve with the radishes, avocado, cotija, cilantro, and lime wedges.

TIP: Roasting the tomatillos before blending them makes the salsa verde extra flavorful. You can roast them whole by placing them on a baking sheet under the broiler for 10 to 15 minutes, or until the skin is blackened in spots.

Per Serving (without garnish): Calories: 251; Protein: 22g; Fat: 8g; Saturated Fat: 1.5g; Carbohydrates: 23g; Sugar: 6.5g; Sodium: 452mg; Fiber: 4.5g

SPICY CHICKEN TORTILLA SOUP

This soup is one of those recipes that is easy to put together, inexpensive, and healthy. The ground chipotle powder adds a fiery punch, but if you don't handle the heat well or are serving this soup to children, just reduce or omit the chipotle powder for a less spicy version. Top it with crispy homemade tortilla strips or store-bought tortilla chips for a delicious soup that can feed your hungry family.

SERVES: 6

PREP TIME: 5 MINUTES

SAUTÉ TIME: 2 MINUTES

PRESSURIZATION TIME:
10 MINUTES

COOK TIME: 10 MINUTES ON
"MANUAL" MODE UNDER HIGH
PRESSURE

RELEASE: QUICK RELEASE

TOTAL TIME: 27 MINUTES

1 tablespoon olive oil

1 onion, diced

4 garlic cloves, minced

1 jalapeño pepper, seeded and diced

2 teaspoons chili powder

1 teaspoon ground cumin

½ teaspoon dried oregano

½ teaspoon ground chipotle powder

4 cups Chicken Broth (page 16) or store-bought unsalted chicken broth

1 pound boneless, skinless chicken breast

1 (15-ounce) can black beans, rinsed and drained

2 (10-ounce) cans diced tomatoes with green chiles

2 cups fresh or frozen corn kernels

Salt

Freshly ground black pepper

Tortilla strips (see Tip, page 95) or tortilla chips, for serving

Diced avocado, for serving

Freshly chopped cilantro, for serving

Lime wedges, for serving

1. Turn on the electric pressure cooker and select the "Sauté" mode. Heat the olive oil and cook the onion and garlic for 2 minutes, or until the onion is soft. Turn off the "Sauté" mode.

2. Add the jalapeño pepper, chili powder, cumin, oregano, chipotle powder, broth, chicken breast, beans, diced tomatoes and green chiles with their juices, and corn, and stir to combine.

3. Secure the lid. Select the "Manual" mode, and set the cooking time for 10 minutes under High Pressure. When the cooking cycle is complete, quick release any remaining steam.

4. Remove the chicken, shred it with two forks, and return it to the soup.

5. Season with salt and pepper to taste. Serve with the tortilla strips, avocado, cilantro, and lime wedges.

TIP: To make the crispy tortilla strips, cut six (6-inch) corn tortillas into ¼-inch strips and toss them with 1 tablespoon of olive oil and ½ teaspoon of salt. Place them on a baking sheet and bake at 350°F for 10 minutes, or until golden brown and crisp. Remove the chips from oven and let them cool completely on the baking sheet before serving.

Per Serving (without garnish): Calories: 217; Protein: 25g; Fat: 4.5g; Saturated Fat: 1g; Carbohydrates: 19g; Sugar: 4g; Sodium: 631mg; Fiber: 5.5g

MEXICAN-STYLE CHICKEN CORN CHOWDER

I have a serious soft spot for corn soup; it's one of my favorites. I usually prefer not to detract from the naturally sweet deliciousness of fresh corn. This chowder is one exception, though. It's a spin on the classic corn chowder with lots of bold flavors. We often pick up a rotisserie chicken from the market, and this is a great way to use it while bringing fresh vegetables and other pantry staples into the mix.

SERVES: 6

PREP TIME: 5 MINUTES

SAUTÉ TIME: 5 MINUTES

PRESSURIZATION TIME: 10 MINUTES

COOK TIME: 5 MINUTES ON "MANUAL" MODE UNDER HIGH PRESSURE

RELEASE: QUICK RELEASE

TOTAL TIME: 25 MINUTES

1½ tablespoons olive oil

1 onion, diced

1 red bell pepper, seeded and diced

3 garlic cloves, minced

2 teaspoons chili powder

1½ teaspoons ground cumin

4 cups Chicken Broth (page 16) or store-bought unsalted chicken broth

1 (7-ounce) can diced green chiles, rinsed and drained

1 (15-ounce) can diced fire-roasted tomatoes

3 cups fresh or frozen corn kernels

2 cups cooked chicken breast or rotisserie chicken, diced

2 tablespoons cornstarch

1 cup half-and-half

Salt

Freshly ground black pepper

1. Turn on the electric pressure cooker and select the "Sauté" mode. Heat the olive oil and cook the onion, bell pepper, and garlic for 4 minutes, or until the vegetables are soft. Turn off the "Sauté" mode.

2. Add the chili powder, cumin, broth, green chiles, diced tomatoes with their juices, corn, and chicken breast, and stir to combine.

3. Secure the lid. Select the "Manual" mode, and set the cooking time for 5 minutes under High Pressure. When the cooking cycle is complete, quick release any remaining steam.

4. In a separate bowl, whisk together the cornstarch and half-and-half. Select the "Sauté" mode again and bring the soup to a simmer. Then, add the cornstarch mixture and stir for 1 minute, or until the soup has thickened. Turn the electric pressure cooker off.

5. Season with salt and pepper to taste.

TIP: If you're using frozen corn, look for fire-roasted corn in the frozen vegetable section of your grocery store. It lends a nice smoky quality to the final product.

Per Serving: Calories: 274; Protein: 20g; Fat: 10g; Saturated Fat: 4g; Carbohydrates: 27g; Sugar: 11g; Sodium: 434mg; Fiber: 3.5g

THAI-INSPIRED RED CURRY CHICKEN NOODLE SOUP

45 MINUTES OR LESS, DAIRY-FREE, GLUTEN-FREE

Here is my twist on the classic Thai-inspired red curry in the form of a comforting chicken noodle soup. The recipe takes one easy shortcut, but the soup still tastes scrumptiously authentic and homemade. Instead of making red curry paste from scratch, I use a good-quality store-bought paste and finish it with lots of fresh herbs. Add a touch more lime juice before serving if you like, which will instantly brighten the flavor of the soup and add a tasty tang to every bite.

SERVES: 4

PREP TIME: 5 MINUTES

SAUTÉ TIME: 7 MINUTES

PRESSURIZATION TIME: 12 MINUTES

COOK TIME: 10 MINUTES ON "MANUAL" MODE UNDER HIGH PRESSURE

RELEASE: QUICK RELEASE

TOTAL TIME: 34 MINUTES

1 tablespoon vegetable oil

2 shallots, sliced

2 garlic cloves, minced

1 teaspoon freshly grated ginger

¼ cup red curry paste

1 tablespoon fish sauce

1 lemongrass stalk (yellow part only), cut into 2-inch sections

1 pound boneless, skinless chicken breast or thighs

6 cups Chicken Broth (page 16) or store-bought unsalted chicken broth

1 (14-ounce) can coconut milk

1 tablespoon brown sugar

1 tablespoon fresh lime juice

1 red bell pepper, seeded and sliced

1 zucchini or summer squash, sliced

8 ounces dried thin rice noodles or vermicelli

Salt

Freshly chopped cilantro, for garnish

Freshly chopped Thai basil, for garnish

Lime wedges, for garnish

1. Turn on the electric pressure cooker and select the "Sauté" mode. Heat the vegetable oil and cook the shallots for 1 minute, or until they are soft. Add the garlic, ginger, and curry paste and cook for 1 minute, or until fragrant. Turn off the "Sauté" mode.

2. Add the fish sauce, lemongrass, chicken breast, and broth, and stir to combine.

3. Secure the lid. Select the "Manual" mode, and set the cooking time for 10 minutes under High Pressure. When the cooking cycle is complete, quick release any remaining steam.

4. Remove and discard the lemongrass stalks.

5. Remove the chicken and shred it with two forks.

6. Select the "Sauté" mode again and bring the soup to a simmer. Then, stir in the coconut milk, brown sugar, lime juice, bell pepper, zucchini, rice noodles, and shredded chicken, and simmer for 5 minutes, or until the vegetables are softened and the noodles are tender. Turn the electric pressure cooker off.

7. Season with salt to taste. Garnish with cilantro, basil, and lime wedges before serving.

TIP: Different red curry pastes have different heat levels. Some can be on the spicier side. Give it a taste before adding it to the soup; you can always add more later. Substitute with extra-firm tofu and vegetable broth for a vegan version of this noodle soup.

Per Serving: Calories: 511; Protein: 36g; Fat: 10g; Saturated Fat: 3.5g; Carbohydrates: 67g; Sugar: 14g; Sodium: 1,664mg; Fiber: 4.5g

TORTELLINI EN BRODO

45 MINUTES OR LESS

This Italian-style minimalist soup, with its clear chicken stock and cheese-stuffed pockets, is as classic as soup gets. I like to use my homemade Chicken Stock (see page 18) and cook it with a piece of Parmesan rind to add flavor. When you finish off a piece of Parmesan, just keep the rind in the freezer so you always have it on hand when you need it. Some cheese shops or grocery stores sell the rinds for a low price.

SERVES: 4

PREP TIME: 5 MINUTES

SAUTÉ TIME: 10 MINUTES

PRESSURIZATION TIME: 12 MINUTES

COOK TIME: 5 MINUTES ON "MANUAL" MODE UNDER HIGH PRESSURE

RELEASE: QUICK RELEASE

TOTAL TIME: 32 MINUTES

6 cups Chicken Stock (page 18) or good-quality store-bought unsalted chicken stock

1 Parmesan rind

12 ounces dried tortellini (any variety)

Salt

Freshly ground black pepper

Grated Parmesan, for serving

1. Place the chicken stock and Parmesan rind in the inner pot of the pressure cooker.

2. Secure the lid. Select the "Manual" mode, and set the cooking time for 5 minutes under High Pressure. When the cooking cycle is complete, quick release any remaining steam.

3. Remove and discard the Parmesan rind.

4. Select the "Sauté" mode. Stir in the tortellini and allow the soup to simmer for 10 minutes, or until the pasta rises to the surface and is tender but still firm to the bite. Turn the electric pressure cooker off.

5. Season with salt and pepper to taste. Sprinkle with grated Parmesan.

TIP: Tortellini cooking times vary greatly, so adjust the cooking time accordingly, depending on the size and whether it is fresh, dried, or frozen. If you think you'll want to save the soup as leftovers, cook the tortellini separately, drain it, and add it to individual bowls just before serving.

Per Serving (without garnish): Calories: 359; Protein: 22g; Fat: 11g; Saturated Fat: 3.5g; Carbohydrates: 49g; Sugar: 3g; Sodium: 697mg; Fiber: 6g

CHICKEN AND POBLANO WHITE CHILI

Chili is one of the most flexible dishes you can prepare no matter your cooking skill level. I love that this chili is a complete "dump-it-and-forget-it" meal made with ingredients that you probably have in your pantry or fridge already. You just throw all the ingredients into the electric pressure cooker and let the delicious flavors develop on their own. As far as toppings go, the more the better, in my opinion, but it would also be delicious if you like to keep it simple with just some crushed tortilla chips.

SERVES: 6

PREP TIME: 5 MINUTES

PRESSURIZATION TIME:
10 MINUTES

COOK TIME: 7 MINUTES ON
"MANUAL" MODE UNDER HIGH
PRESSURE

RELEASE: NATURAL RELEASE FOR
10 MINUTES, THEN QUICK RELEASE

TOTAL TIME: 32 MINUTES

1 onion, diced

3 garlic cloves, minced

2 poblano peppers, seeded
and chopped

1 jalapeño pepper, seeded
and diced

1 teaspoon ground cumin

1 teaspoon dried oregano

½ teaspoon ground coriander

¼ teaspoon cayenne pepper

2 (15-ounce) cans cannellini
beans, rinsed and drained

2 cups cooked chicken breast or
rotisserie chicken, diced

4 cups Chicken Broth (page 16)
or store-bought unsalted
chicken broth

Salt

Freshly ground black pepper

Freshly chopped cilantro,
for serving

Diced avocado, for serving

Tortilla chips, for serving

1. Place the onion, garlic, poblano peppers, jalapeño pepper, cumin, oregano, coriander, cayenne pepper, beans, chicken breast, and broth in the inner pot of the pressure cooker, and stir to combine.

2. Secure the lid. Select the "Manual" mode, and set the cooking time for 7 minutes under High Pressure. When the cooking cycle is complete, natural release for 10 minutes, then quick release any remaining steam. Turn the electric pressure cooker off.

3. Season with salt and pepper to taste. Serve with the cilantro, avocado, and tortilla chips.

TIP: If cooked chicken is not readily available, you can use raw diced chicken breast. Just increase the cooking time to 10 minutes under High Pressure, natural release for 10 minutes, then quick release any remaining steam.

Per Serving (without garnish): Calories: 226; Protein: 25g; Fat: 1.5g; Saturated Fat: 0.5g; Carbohydrates: 28g; Sugar: 4.5g; Sodium: 511mg; Fiber: 8g

GREEK-STYLE AVGOLEMONO SOUP

45 MINUTES OR LESS, DAIRY-FREE, GLUTEN-FREE

Avgolemono differs from almost any other chicken soup. It's velvety and luxurious thanks to the eggs added at the end, which result in extra richness, while the tart lemon brings a bright finish. The trick to getting that silky texture is to add a little of the hot broth to the eggs to temper them before adding to the pot of soup, so that you get a nice smooth soup rather than strings of eggs throughout.

SERVES: 4

PREP TIME: 5 MINUTES

SAUTÉ TIME: 5 MINUTES

PRESSURIZATION TIME: 12 MINUTES

COOK TIME: 15 MINUTES ON "MANUAL" MODE UNDER HIGH PRESSURE

RELEASE: QUICK RELEASE

TOTAL TIME: 37 MINUTES

1 tablespoon olive oil

1 onion, diced

2 garlic cloves, minced

2 celery stalks, diced

1 bay leaf

½ cup uncooked long-grain white rice

1 pound boneless, skinless chicken breast

5 cups Chicken Broth (page 16) or store-bought unsalted chicken broth

2 large eggs

2 tablespoons fresh lemon juice

Salt

Freshly ground black pepper

Freshly chopped dill, for serving

1. Turn on the electric pressure cooker and select the "Sauté" mode. Heat the olive oil and cook the onion, garlic, and celery for 4 minutes, or until the vegetables are soft. Turn off the "Sauté" mode.

2. Add the bay leaf, rice, chicken breast, and broth, and stir to combine.

3. Secure the lid. Select the "Manual" mode, and set the cooking time for 15 minutes under High Pressure. When the cooking cycle is complete, quick release any remaining steam.

4. Remove and discard the bay leaf.

5. Remove the chicken and shred it with two forks.

6. In a medium bowl, whisk together the eggs and lemon juice. Slowly ladle 1 cup of hot soup into the egg mixture and whisk until combined.

7. Select the "Sauté" mode again and bring the soup to a simmer. Then, stir in the shredded chicken and slowly pour the egg mixture back into the pot, stirring constantly. Simmer for 1 minute, or until the soup has thickened. Turn the electric pressure cooker off.

8. Season with salt and pepper to taste. Garnish with fresh dill before serving.

TIP: For a richer, creamier soup, use three egg yolks instead of two whole eggs.

Per Serving: Calories: 329; Protein: 35g; Fat: 9g; Saturated Fat: 2g; Carbohydrates: 25g; Sugar: 3g; Sodium: 261mg; Fiber: 1g

CHICKEN PARMESAN SOUP

A quick and delicious weeknight-friendly meal, this soup is a great way to use up your leftover roasted chicken. It has all the flavors of chicken Parmesan cooked up conveniently in a soup form, and it will quickly become a family favorite. Pair it with a green salad and garlic bread, and you're all set for a great dinner!

SERVES: 6

PREP TIME: 5 MINUTES

SAUTÉ TIME: 2 MINUTES

PRESSURIZATION TIME: 12 MINUTES

COOK TIME: 5 MINUTES ON "MANUAL" MODE UNDER HIGH PRESSURE

RELEASE: QUICK RELEASE

TOTAL TIME: 24 MINUTES

1 tablespoon olive oil

1 onion, diced

3 garlic cloves, minced

1½ teaspoons Italian seasoning

¼ teaspoon red pepper flakes

¼ cup tomato paste

1 (28-ounce) can diced tomatoes

2 cups uncooked rotini or penne

2 cups cooked chicken breast or rotisserie chicken, diced

5 cups Chicken Broth (page 16) or store-bought unsalted chicken broth

½ cup shredded mozzarella

½ cup shredded Parmesan, plus more for serving

Salt

Freshly ground black pepper

Freshly chopped basil, for serving

1. Turn on the electric pressure cooker and select the "Sauté" mode. Heat the olive oil and cook the onion and garlic for 2 minutes, or until the onion is soft. Turn off the "Sauté" mode.

2. Add the Italian seasoning, red pepper flakes, tomato paste, diced tomatoes with their juices, rotini, chicken breast, and broth, and stir to combine.

3. Secure the lid. Select the "Manual" mode, and set the cooking time for 5 minutes under High Pressure. When the cooking cycle is complete, quick release any remaining steam.

4. Stir in the shredded mozzarella and Parmesan and season with salt and pepper to taste. Serve with the basil and additional Parmesan.

TIP: Grating mozzarella and Parmesan yourself is always best, but you can also substitute 1 cup of Italian-style shredded cheese blend for convenience.

Per Serving: Calories: 330; Protein: 27g; Fat: 8.5g; Saturated Fat: 3g; Carbohydrates: 36g; Sugar: 7.5g; Sodium: 637mg; Fiber: 3.5g

INDIAN-STYLE CHICKEN AND LENTIL SOUP (MULLIGATAWNY)

45 MINUTES OR LESS, FREEZER-FRIENDLY, GLUTEN-FREE

Mulligatawny is a curried chicken and red lentil soup seasoned with a blend of Indian spices for a complex and delightful taste. My mother-in-law Patti first introduced me to this delicious soup and I knew I wanted to make a quicker electric pressure cooker version with the same flavor and texture. Finishing the soup with some diced apples at the end gives it a surprising crunch and a burst of sweet tartness. Some recipes call for blending the soup into a puree, but I prefer a chunky consistency, which is particularly tasty when served with warm naan bread or cooked basmati rice.

SERVES: 6
PREP TIME: 5 MINUTES
SAUTÉ TIME: 5 MINUTES
PRESSURIZATION TIME:
10 MINUTES
COOK TIME: 15 MINUTES ON
"MANUAL" MODE UNDER HIGH
PRESSURE
RELEASE: QUICK RELEASE
TOTAL TIME: 35 MINUTES

2 tablespoons unsalted butter

1 onion, diced

3 garlic cloves, minced

2 teaspoons freshly grated ginger

1½ tablespoons curry powder

1 teaspoon ground coriander

½ teaspoon turmeric

½ teaspoon ground cumin

2 carrots, peeled and diced

1 celery stalk, diced

½ cup dried red lentils, rinsed
and drained

8 ounces boneless, skinless
chicken breast, cut into
bite-size pieces

4 cups Chicken Broth (page 16) or
store-bought unsalted
chicken broth

1 apple, peeled, cored, and diced

1 (14-ounce) can coconut milk

Salt

Freshly ground black pepper

1. Turn on the electric pressure cooker and select the "Sauté" mode. Melt the butter and cook the onion for 2 minutes, or until soft. Add the garlic, ginger, curry powder, coriander, turmeric, and cumin and cook for 1 minute or until the spices are fragrant. Turn off the "Sauté" mode.

2. Add the carrots, celery, lentils, chicken breast, and broth, and stir to combine.

3. Secure the lid. Select the "Manual" mode, and set the cooking time for 15 minutes under High Pressure. When the cooking cycle is complete, quick release any remaining steam.

4. Select the "Sauté" mode again and bring the soup to a simmer. Then, stir in the apple and coconut milk and cook for 2 minutes. Turn the electric pressure cooker off.

5. Season with salt and pepper to taste.

TIP: Granny Smith apples are generally the preferred variety for this soup, but if you like a less tart flavor, Gala would be a good alternative.

Per Serving: Calories: 313; Protein: 16g; Fat: 19g; Saturated Fat: 15g; Carbohydrates: 21g; Sugar: 5.5g; Sodium: 131mg; Fiber: 4g

CHICKEN SOBA NOODLE SOUP WITH BOK CHOY AND GINGER

45 MINUTES OR LESS, DAIRY-FREE

Soba is a Japanese-style noodle made from buckwheat flour with a texture and flavor similar to whole wheat pasta. Soba noodles and chicken breast tenders are cooked in a savory broth infused with garlic and ginger for subtle heat. Using an umami-rich dashi broth gives this noodle soup more body and a completely different character, but making it with chicken broth is just as soothing and nourishing. If you don't have bok choy on hand, try it with baby spinach or napa cabbage.

SERVES: 4

PREP TIME: 10 MINUTES

SAUTÉ TIME: 4 MINUTES

PRESSURIZATION TIME: 12 MINUTES

COOK TIME: 5 MINUTES ON "MANUAL" MODE UNDER HIGH PRESSURE

RELEASE: QUICK RELEASE

TOTAL TIME: 31 MINUTES

6 ounces dried soba noodles

1 teaspoon vegetable oil

2 garlic cloves, minced

1 teaspoon freshly grated ginger

8 ounces chicken breast tenders, thinly sliced

6 cups Dashi Broth (page 17) or Chicken Broth (page 16) or store-bought unsalted dashi or chicken broth

¼ cup low-sodium soy sauce

8 ounces baby bok choy, ends trimmed and chopped into bite-size pieces

Salt

continued >

CHICKEN SOBA NOODLE SOUP WITH BOK CHOY AND GINGER

continued

1. Cook the noodles according to the package directions and rinse them with cold water. Drain well and set aside.

2. Turn on the electric pressure cooker and select the "Sauté" mode. Heat the vegetable oil and cook the garlic and ginger for 1 minute, or until fragrant. Turn off the "Sauté" mode.

3. Add the chicken breast tenders and broth, and stir to combine.

4. Secure the lid. Select the "Manual" mode, and set the cooking time for 5 minutes under High Pressure. When the cooking cycle is complete, quick release any remaining steam.

5. Select the "Sauté" mode again. Stir in the soy sauce and bok choy and bring to a simmer. Allow the soup to simmer for 3 minutes, or until the vegetables are soft. Add the cooked noodles and stir until heated through. Turn the electric pressure cooker off and season with salt to taste.

TIP: Dashi, a Japanese-style broth, is full of flavor and worth the extra effort to obtain the three ingredients needed to make it (see page 17). Some Asian grocery stores carry instant dashi powder, which is used similarly to chicken bouillon and can be a convenient option if you don't want to make a full batch of dashi from scratch.

Per Serving: Calories: 257; Protein: 26g; Fat: 3g; Saturated Fat: 0.5g; Carbohydrates: 37g; Sugar: 0.5g; Sodium: 784mg; Fiber: 3g

CAJUN-STYLE TURKEY AND RED BEAN SOUP

DAIRY-FREE, FREEZER-FRIENDLY, GLUTEN-FREE

Red beans and rice is a Cajun-style dish traditionally prepped and served on Monday, or laundry day. The idea is that the pot of red beans can sit on the stove and simmer away all day while the laundry is being tended to. Using the electric pressure cooker, this meal requires very little hands-on attention, leaving you plenty of time to handle any chore any day of the week. Serve this soup with some skillet cornbread on the side and Louisiana-style hot sauce for a little kick.

SERVES: 6

PREP TIME: 5 MINUTES

SAUTÉ TIME: 4 MINUTES

PRESSURIZATION TIME: 12 MINUTES

COOK TIME: 35 MINUTES ON "MANUAL" MODE UNDER HIGH PRESSURE

RELEASE: NATURAL RELEASE FOR 15 MINUTES, THEN QUICK RELEASE

TOTAL TIME: 1 HOUR 11 MINUTES

1 tablespoon olive oil

1 onion, diced

1 green bell pepper, seeded and diced

2 celery stalks, diced

2 garlic cloves, minced

1 pound smoked turkey wings or leg

1 pound dried red kidney beans, soaked overnight, rinsed, and drained

2 teaspoons salt-free Cajun seasoning

2 bay leaves

5 cups water

Salt

Freshly ground black pepper

Cooked white rice, for serving

Sliced scallions, for serving

Hot sauce, for serving

continued >

CAJUN-STYLE TURKEY AND RED BEAN SOUP

continued

1. Turn on the electric pressure cooker and select the "Sauté" mode. Heat the olive oil and cook the onion, bell pepper, celery, and garlic for 4 minutes, or until the vegetables are soft. Turn off the "Sauté" mode.

2. Add the turkey wings, beans, Cajun seasoning, bay leaves, and water, and stir to combine.

3. Secure the lid. Select the "Manual" mode, and set the cooking time for 35 minutes under High Pressure. When the cooking cycle is complete, natural release for 15 minutes, then quick release any remaining steam.

4. Remove and discard the bay leaves and turkey wing. If using turkey leg, remove the tender meat, chop it into smaller pieces, and add it to the soup.

5. Using an immersion blender, traditional blender, or food processor, partially blend the soup if you desire a thicker consistency. Season it with salt and pepper to taste. Serve with the rice, scallions, and hot sauce.

TIP: For a quick-cooking version, substitute sliced smoked turkey sausage for the turkey wings, two (15-ounce) cans of red kidney beans for the dried beans, and reduce the cooking time to 8 minutes with quick release after cooking.

Per Serving (without rice): Calories: 295; Protein: 22g; Fat: 4g; Saturated Fat: 1g; Carbohydrates: 44g; Sugar: 2g; Sodium: 204mg; Fiber: 12g

CREAMY TURKEY AND WILD RICE SOUP

Perfect for a cool autumn day when you're craving something cozy and filling, this soup couldn't be easier to make. The turkey is cooked to tender perfection while the mushrooms infuse the soup with their earthy flavor, and the wild rice absorbs the liquid as it cooks.

SERVES: 4

PREP TIME: 5 MINUTES

SAUTÉ TIME: 1 MINUTE

PRESSURIZATION TIME:
10 MINUTES

COOK TIME: 35 MINUTES ON "MANUAL" MODE UNDER HIGH PRESSURE

RELEASE: QUICK RELEASE

TOTAL TIME: 51 MINUTES

1 onion, diced

3 garlic cloves, minced

2 carrots, peeled and diced

2 celery stalks, diced

2 thyme sprigs

1 bay leaf

8 ounces white button mushrooms, sliced

1 cup uncooked wild rice, rinsed and drained

1 pound boneless, skinless turkey breast

4 cups Chicken Broth (page 16) or store-bought unsalted turkey or chicken broth

1 tablespoon cornstarch

¾ cup half-and-half

Salt

Freshly ground black pepper

continued >

CREAMY TURKEY AND WILD RICE SOUP

continued

1. Place the onion, garlic, carrots, celery, thyme, bay leaf, mushrooms, rice, turkey breast, and broth in the inner pot of the pressure cooker, and stir to combine.

2. Secure the lid. Select the "Manual" mode, and set the cooking time for 35 minutes under High Pressure. When the cooking cycle is complete, quick release any remaining steam.

3. Remove and discard the thyme sprigs and bay leaf.

4. Remove the turkey and shred it with two forks.

5. In a separate bowl, whisk together the cornstarch and half-and-half. Select the "Sauté" mode and bring the soup to a simmer. Then, add the cornstarch mixture and stir for 1 minute, or until the soup has thickened. Stir in the shredded turkey and turn the electric pressure cooker off.

6. Season with salt and pepper to taste.

TIP: You can modify this recipe by substituting barley or farro for the wild rice.

Per Serving: Calories: 373; Protein: 39g; Fat: 6g; Saturated Fat: 3g; Carbohydrates: 44g; Sugar: 6.5g; Sodium: 532mg; Fiber: 4.5g

TURKEY PUMPKIN CHILI

45 MINUTES OR LESS, FREEZER-FRIENDLY, GLUTEN-FREE

Most of the ingredients in this chili are basic pantry staples, making it a snap to put together. It has a blend of warm spices with a touch of heat and smokiness from the chipotle pepper, which adds a complex dimension of flavor. The addition of pumpkin puree lends a subtle sweetness and creamy texture to this chili—a great way to sneak more veggies into the diet for kids (and adults)!

SERVES: 4

PREP TIME: 5 MINUTES

SAUTÉ TIME: 7 MINUTES

PRESSURIZATION TIME: 10 MINUTES

COOK TIME: 15 MINUTES ON "MANUAL" MODE UNDER HIGH PRESSURE

RELEASE: QUICK RELEASE

TOTAL TIME: 37 MINUTES

1 tablespoon olive oil

1 pound ground turkey

1 onion, diced

3 garlic cloves, minced

1 chipotle pepper in adobo sauce, minced

1 teaspoon chili powder

1½ tablespoons ground cumin

½ teaspoon dried oregano

1 cup fresh or frozen corn kernels

2 (15-ounce) cans black beans, rinsed and drained

1 (15-ounce) can crushed tomatoes

1 (15-ounce) can pumpkin puree

2 cups Chicken Broth (page 16) or store-bought unsalted turkey or chicken broth

Salt

Freshly ground black pepper

Sliced scallions, for serving

Shredded cheese, for serving

Tortilla chips, for serving

Sour cream, for serving

continued >

TURKEY PUMPKIN CHILI

continued

1. Turn on the electric pressure cooker and select the "Sauté" mode. Heat the olive oil and cook the ground turkey, breaking up large pieces into small crumbles, for 5 minutes, or until browned. Add the onion and garlic and cook for 2 minutes, or until the onion is soft. Turn off the "Sauté" mode.

2. Add the chipotle pepper, chili powder, cumin, oregano, corn, beans, crushed tomatoes, pumpkin puree, and broth, and stir to combine.

3. Secure the lid. Select the "Manual" mode, and set the cooking time for 15 minutes under High Pressure. When the cooking cycle is complete, quick release any remaining steam. Turn the electric pressure cooker off.

4. Season the soup with salt and pepper to taste. Serve with the scallions, shredded cheese, tortilla chips, and sour cream.

TIP: Letting the chili refrigerate overnight and then reheating it gently allows flavors to mingle and makes this good dish even better. When reheating it, you may need to add a bit more broth or water if it becomes too thick.

Per Serving (without garnish): Calories: 528; Protein: 40g; Fat: 14g; Saturated Fat: 3g; Carbohydrates: 63g; Sugar: 12g; Sodium: 824mg; Fiber: 20g

DAY-AFTER-THANKSGIVING TURKEY AND VEGETABLE SOUP

Rather than the usual leftover turkey sandwich after Thanksgiving, try taking advantage of that turkey carcass to make a quick stock (see Chicken Stock, page 18) to use as a base for this soup. I love that it's loaded with fresh vegetables, which will make you forget all the excesses from the day before.

SERVES: 6

PREP TIME: 5 MINUTES

PRESSURIZATION TIME: 12 MINUTES

COOK TIME: 8 MINUTES ON "MANUAL" MODE UNDER HIGH PRESSURE

RELEASE: QUICK RELEASE

TOTAL TIME: 25 MINUTES

1 onion, diced

3 garlic cloves, minced

2 carrots, peeled and diced

1 celery stalk, diced

1 zucchini, diced

1 large sweet potato, peeled and diced

2 tablespoons tomato paste

½ teaspoon Italian seasoning

2 cups cooked turkey meat, diced

5 cups Chicken Stock (page 18) or store-bought unsalted turkey or chicken stock

Salt

Freshly ground black pepper

Freshly chopped flat-leaf parsley, for garnish

continued >

DAY-AFTER-THANKSGIVING TURKEY AND VEGETABLE SOUP

continued

1. Place the onion, garlic, carrots, celery, zucchini, sweet potato, tomato paste, Italian seasoning, turkey meat, and stock in the inner pot of the pressure cooker, and stir to combine.

2. Secure the lid. Select the "Manual" mode, and set the cooking time for 8 minutes under High Pressure. When the cooking cycle is complete, quick release any remaining steam. Turn the electric pressure cooker off.

3. Season with salt and pepper to taste. Garnish with fresh parsley before serving.

TIP: This soup is a good way to incorporate any leftover vegetable sides you may have from your holiday meal, such as green beans, corn, and sweet potatoes. Simply select the "Sauté" mode after the cooking cycle is complete, stir in the cooked vegetables (preferably cut up into bite-size pieces), and simmer until heated through.

Per Serving: Calories: 150; Protein: 15g; Fat: 2g; Saturated Fat: 0.5g; Carbohydrates: 19g; Sugar: 5.5g; Sodium: 580mg; Fiber: 3.5g

ITALIAN-STYLE WEDDING SOUP WITH TURKEY MEATBALLS

45 MINUTES OR LESS, FREEZER-FRIENDLY

One of my all-time favorite one-pot meals, this light, healthy soup has a good balance of meatballs, vegetables, and pasta. It really is perfect for any time of the year. Sometimes, turkey meatballs can taste a little dry and bland, which is why I stay away from extra-lean ground turkey and opt for one with a higher fat content. It would also be a lot of fun to make these into mini meatballs with alphabet pasta for kids!

SERVES: 6

PREP TIME: 10 MINUTES

SAUTÉ TIME: 16 MINUTES

PRESSURIZATION TIME: 12 MINUTES

COOK TIME: 5 MINUTES ON "MANUAL" MODE UNDER HIGH PRESSURE

RELEASE: QUICK RELEASE

TOTAL TIME: 43 MINUTES

FOR THE MEATBALLS

1 pound ground turkey (preferably 93% lean)

1 large egg

1 teaspoon salt

¼ teaspoon freshly ground black pepper

½ teaspoon Italian seasoning

½ teaspoon garlic powder

⅓ cup panko or plain bread crumbs

⅓ cup grated Parmesan

2 tablespoons freshly chopped parsley

2 tablespoons olive oil

FOR THE SOUP

1 onion, diced

2 carrots, peeled and diced

1 celery stalk, diced

6 cups Chicken Broth (page 16) or store-bought unsalted turkey or chicken broth

1 cup uncooked orzo or acini de pepe

2 cups baby spinach leaves

Salt

Freshly ground black pepper

continued >

ITALIAN-STYLE WEDDING SOUP WITH TURKEY MEATBALLS

continued

TO MAKE THE MEATBALLS

1. In a large bowl, mix together the ground turkey, egg, salt, pepper, Italian seasoning, garlic powder, bread crumbs, Parmesan, and parsley. Shape the mixture into small (1-inch) meatballs.

2. Turn on the electric pressure cooker and select the "Sauté" mode. Heat the olive oil and cook the meatballs for 3 minutes per side, or until browned. Set aside.

TO MAKE THE SOUP

3. Place the onion, carrots, celery, and broth in the inner pot of the pressure cooker, and stir to combine.

4. Secure the lid. Select the "Manual" mode, and set the cooking time for 5 minutes under High Pressure. When the cooking cycle is complete, quick release any remaining steam.

5. Select the "Sauté" mode and bring the soup to a simmer. Then, stir in the orzo and meatballs and cook for 10 minutes, or until the pasta is tender. Stir in the spinach and cook until wilted. Turn the electric pressure cooker off.

6. Season with salt and pepper to taste.

TIP: Be gentle when handling the meatball mixture and don't overmix it; packing the meat too tightly will make the meatballs tough and chewy. When shaping the meatballs, lightly oil your hands to prevent the meat mixture from sticking.

Per Serving: Calories: 333; Protein: 5g; Fat: 13g; Saturated Fat: 3.5g; Carbohydrates: 30g; Sugar: 4g; Sodium: 796mg; Fiber: 2.5g

SOUTHWESTERN TURKEY SOUP

It's always nice to be able to make a delicious meal without spending a lot of time in the kitchen, and this straightforward recipe proves that it's absolutely possible. Bring the flavors of Southwestern-style cuisine to your dinner table with this quick and easy meal that the whole family will love.

SERVES: 6

PREP TIME: 5 MINUTES

SAUTÉ TIME: 7 MINUTES

PRESSURIZATION TIME: 10 MINUTES

COOK TIME: 5 MINUTES ON "MANUAL" MODE UNDER HIGH PRESSURE

RELEASE: NATURAL RELEASE FOR 10 MINUTES, THEN QUICK RELEASE

TOTAL TIME: 37 MINUTES

1 tablespoon olive oil

1 pound ground turkey

1 onion, diced

3 garlic cloves, minced

1 green bell pepper, seeded and diced

1 tablespoon chili powder

1 teaspoon paprika

1 teaspoon ground cumin

1 (10-ounce) can diced tomatoes with green chiles

1 (15-ounce) can red kidney beans, rinsed and drained

4 cups Chicken Broth (page 16) or store-bought unsalted turkey or chicken broth

4 ounces cream cheese

Salt

Freshly ground black pepper

Freshly chopped cilantro, for serving

Tortilla chips, for serving

Lime wedges, for serving

continued >

SOUTHWESTERN TURKEY SOUP

continued

1. Turn on the electric pressure cooker and select the "Sauté" mode. Heat the olive oil and cook the ground turkey, breaking up large pieces into small crumbles, for 5 minutes, or until browned. Add the onion and garlic and cook for 2 minutes, or until the onion is soft. Turn off the "Sauté" mode.

2. Add the bell pepper, chili powder, paprika, cumin, diced tomatoes and green chiles with their juices, beans, and broth, and stir to combine.

3. Secure the lid. Select the "Manual" mode, and set the cooking time for 5 minutes under High Pressure. When the cooking cycle is complete, natural release for 10 minutes, then quick release any remaining steam.

4. Select the "Sauté" mode again and bring the soup to a simmer. Then, stir in the cream cheese and cook until it is incorporated and heated through. Turn the electric pressure cooker off.

5. Season with salt and pepper to taste. Serve with the cilantro, tortilla chips, and lime wedges.

TIP: The recipe is not very spicy as it is, but if you prefer a little more heat, you can add a 4-ounce can of diced green chiles when adding the bell pepper.

Per Serving (without garnish): Calories: 288; Protein: 22g; Fat: 15g; Saturated Fat: 5.5g; Carbohydrates: 18g; Sugar: 3.5g; Sodium: 664mg; Fiber: 4.5g

TURKEY ENCHILADA SOUP

If you're looking for a convenient way to eat enchiladas without the mess of assembling and baking them, this tasty soup is exactly what you're looking for. This deconstructed dish gives you all the enchilada flavor you want in a fraction of the time.

SERVES: 6

PREP TIME: 5 MINUTES

SAUTÉ TIME: 3 MINUTES

PRESSURIZATION TIME: 10 MINUTES

COOK TIME: 7 MINUTES ON "MANUAL" MODE UNDER HIGH PRESSURE

RELEASE: QUICK RELEASE

TOTAL TIME: 25 MINUTES

1 tablespoon olive oil

1 onion, diced

3 garlic cloves, minced

1 teaspoon ground cumin

1 (10-ounce) can red enchilada sauce

1 (15-ounce) can black beans, rinsed and drained

1 (15-ounce) can diced fire-roasted tomatoes

2 cups cooked turkey breast, shredded

4 cups Chicken Broth (page 16) or store-bought unsalted turkey or chicken broth, divided

¼ cup masa harina

8 ounces sharp cheddar, shredded

Salt

Freshly ground black pepper

Tortilla strips, for serving

Diced avocado, for serving

Freshly chopped cilantro, for serving

Sour cream, for serving

Lime wedges, for serving

continued >

TURKEY ENCHILADA SOUP

continued

1. Turn on the electric pressure cooker and select the "Sauté" mode. Heat the olive oil and cook the onion and garlic for 2 minutes, or until the onion is soft. Turn off the "Sauté" mode. Add the cumin, enchilada sauce, beans, diced tomatoes with their juices, turkey breast, and 3 cups of the broth, and stir to combine.

2. Secure the lid. Select the "Manual" mode, and set the cooking time for 7 minutes under High Pressure. When the cooking cycle is complete, quick release any remaining steam.

3. In a separate bowl, whisk together the remaining 1 cup of broth and masa harina. Select the "Sauté" mode again and bring the soup to a simmer. Then, add the masa harina mixture and stir for 1 minute, or until the soup has thickened. Add the cheddar and slowly stir until incorporated. Turn the electric pressure cooker off.

4. Season with salt and pepper to taste. Serve with the tortilla strips, avocado, cilantro, sour cream, and lime wedges.

TIP: Masa harina is a fine, powdery cornmeal used as a thickening agent in this soup, giving it a distinctive corn tortilla taste. It can usually be found in the Hispanic food section (or sometimes next to cornmeal) in most major grocery stores. If it's not available, you can thicken the soup with cornstarch instead.

Per Serving (without garnish): Calories: 390; Protein: 34g; Fat: 17g; Saturated Fat: 8g; Carbohydrates: 25g; Sugar: 4.5g; Sodium: 860mg; Fiber: 6.5g

VIETNAMESE-INSPIRED DUCK AND EGG NOODLE SOUP (MI VIT TIEM)

Mi Vit Tiem is a Vietnamese-inspired noodle soup of Chinese origin. The broth is infused with the rich flavors of slow-roasted duck as well as spices and aromatics, giving it a unique and unforgettable taste. Ladled over some egg noodles and bok choy and served with pieces of the roast duck, this is another one of my cold-weather favorites.

SERVES: 4

PREP TIME: 10 MINUTES

SAUTÉ TIME: 3 MINUTES

PRESSURIZATION TIME:
12 MINUTES

COOK TIME: 10 MINUTES ON "MANUAL" MODE UNDER HIGH PRESSURE

RELEASE: QUICK RELEASE

TOTAL TIME: 35 MINUTES

8 ounces fresh or dried egg noodles

Half of a Chinese-style roast duck

1 cinnamon stick

2 star anise

1 (1-inch) piece fresh ginger, sliced

2 garlic cloves, smashed

¼ teaspoon red pepper flakes

6 cups water

2 tablespoons fish sauce

1 tablespoon brown sugar

8 ounces baby bok choy, ends trimmed and chopped into bite-size pieces

Salt

continued >

VIETNAMESE-INSPIRED DUCK AND EGG NOODLE SOUP (MI VIT TIEM)

continued

1. Cook the noodles according to the package directions and rinse them with cold water. Drain well and set aside.

2. Remove the meat from the roast duck and reserve the carcass and its juices. Cut the meat into bite-size pieces and set aside.

3. Place the duck carcass with its juices, cinnamon stick, star anise, ginger, garlic, red pepper flakes, and water in the inner pot of the pressure cooker, and stir to combine.

4. Secure the lid. Select the "Manual" mode, and set the cooking time for 10 minutes under High Pressure. When the cooking cycle is complete, quick release any remaining steam.

5. Select the "Sauté" mode and bring the soup to a simmer. Then, stir in the fish sauce, brown sugar, and bok choy and simmer for 3 minutes, or until the vegetables are soft. Stir in the cooked noodles. Turn the electric pressure cooker off.

6. Season with salt to taste.

TIP: If you can't get your hands on a Chinese-style roast duck, try it with roasted chicken or turkey. It won't taste as rich, but the spices and aromatics will create a delicious soup nevertheless.

Per Serving: Calories: 366; Protein: 32g; Fat: 16g; Saturated Fat: 5.5g; Carbohydrates: 21g; Sugar: 8g; Sodium: 980mg; Fiber: 1.5g

CHAPTER 6

HEARTY MEAT SOUPS AND STEWS

One-dish meals are always welcome at our house, and the recipes in this section highlight the hearty meat soups and stews that are a meal on their own. Rustic, country-style stews like Irish-Inspired Lamb Stew with Stout (page 136) and Spanish-Style Chicken Stew (page 138) make for a satisfying meal at home on a weeknight, while classics such as Smoky Chipotle Beef Brisket Chili (page 162) are excellent for sharing with friends and family when you have company.

Cooking in the electric pressure cooker is perfect for recipes that call for inexpensive cuts of meat like pork shoulder and beef chuck, which require long cooking times to become tender. I like to season the meat with some salt and pepper and give it a good sear at the beginning of the cooking process to build an extra layer of flavor; try not to skip this important step. Also, the browned bits on the bottom of the pot pack a ton of flavor, so be sure to stir all that goodness into the soup when you add the liquid to the pot.

Whether you're making a weeknight dinner for your family or hosting a small dinner party, these recipes won't require much attention, allowing you to set it and forget it without having to worry about watching the stove.

< Irish-Inspired Lamb Stew with Stout, page 136

LAMB AND CHICKPEA STEW

DAIRY-FREE, FREEZER-FRIENDLY

This stew is all about the spices! Reminiscent of the flavors of shawarma, this dish comes packed with exciting Middle Eastern–inspired flavors. Not only does cooking it in the electric pressure cooker save time, it also retains all the flavors and aromas as the chunks of lamb cook to perfect tenderness.

SERVES: 6

PREP TIME: 5 MINUTES

SAUTÉ TIME: 7 MINUTES

PRESSURIZATION TIME: 8 MINUTES

COOK TIME: 40 MINUTES ON "MANUAL" MODE UNDER HIGH PRESSURE

RELEASE: NATURAL RELEASE FOR 10 MINUTES, THEN QUICK RELEASE

TOTAL TIME: 1 HOUR 10 MINUTES

2 tablespoons olive oil

1 pound boneless lamb shoulder, cut into 1-inch pieces

1 onion, diced

2 garlic cloves, minced

2 carrots, peeled and chopped

2 teaspoons ground cumin

1 teaspoon ground coriander

1 teaspoon turmeric

¼ teaspoon ground cinnamon

¼ teaspoon cayenne pepper

1 (15-ounce) can chickpeas, rinsed and drained

1 (15-ounce) can crushed tomatoes

¼ cup raisins

2 cups Chicken Broth (page 16) or store-bought unsalted chicken broth

Salt

Freshly ground black pepper

Freshly chopped cilantro, for garnish

Cooked couscous, for serving

1. Turn on the electric pressure cooker and select the "Sauté" mode. Heat the olive oil and cook the lamb for 5 minutes, or until browned. Add the onion and garlic and cook for 2 minutes, or until the onion is soft. Turn off the "Sauté" mode.

2. Add the carrots, cumin, coriander, turmeric, cinnamon, cayenne pepper, chickpeas, tomatoes, raisins, and broth, and stir to combine.

3. Secure the lid. Select the "Manual" mode, and set the cooking time for 40 minutes under High Pressure. When the cooking cycle is complete, natural release for 10 minutes, then quick release any remaining steam.

4. Season the soup with salt and pepper to taste. Garnish with fresh cilantro and serve over couscous.

TIP: Some stores sell packaged lamb stew meat, which is often made up of different cuts in small pieces. It's best to use the shoulder cut and divide it into 1-inch pieces so they cook evenly. You can ask your butcher for help with the task or for recommendations on alternative lamb cuts if the shoulder is not available.

Per Serving (without couscous): Calories: 289; Protein: 19g; Fat: 11g; Saturated Fat: 3g; Carbohydrates: 28g; Sugar: 12g; Sodium: 365mg; Fiber: 6.5g

HEARTY HAMBURGER SOUP

45 MINUTES OR LESS, DAIRY-FREE, FREEZER-FRIENDLY, GLUTEN-FREE

Typically made with canned tomato soup, this version uses diced tomatoes, so it's a bit healthier and just as good. One of the best things about this recipe is that you can always use whatever fresh vegetables you have instead of the frozen vegetables; fresh spinach, green beans, or zucchini would be good choices.

SERVES: 6

PREP TIME: 5 MINUTES

SAUTÉ TIME: 12 MINUTES

PRESSURIZATION TIME: 12 MINUTES

COOK TIME: 7 MINUTES ON "MANUAL" MODE UNDER HIGH PRESSURE

RELEASE: QUICK RELEASE

TOTAL TIME: 36 MINUTES

1 tablespoon olive oil

1 pound ground beef

1 onion, diced

3 garlic cloves, minced

1 Yukon Gold potato, diced

½ teaspoon dried oregano

1 teaspoon Italian seasoning

1 teaspoon Worcestershire sauce

1 tablespoon tomato paste

1 (15-ounce) can diced tomatoes

5 cups Roasted Beef Bone Stock (page 19) or store-bought unsalted beef broth

2 cups frozen mixed vegetables (carrots, green beans, corn, peas)

Salt

Freshly ground black pepper

1. Turn on the electric pressure cooker and select the "Sauté" mode. Heat the olive oil and cook the beef for 5 minutes, or until browned. Drain off excess grease, leaving about 1 tablespoon of fat in the pot. Add the onion and garlic and cook for 2 minutes, or until the onion is soft. Turn off the "Sauté" mode.

2. Add the potato, oregano, Italian seasoning, Worcestershire sauce, tomato paste, diced tomatoes with their juices, and stock, and stir to combine.

3. Secure the lid. Select the "Manual" mode, and set the cooking time for 7 minutes under High Pressure. When the cooking cycle is complete, quick release any remaining steam.

4. Select the "Sauté" mode again and bring the soup to a simmer. Then, stir in the frozen mixed vegetables and simmer for 5 minutes, or until the vegetables are tender. Turn the electric pressure cooker off.

5. Season with salt and pepper to taste.

TIP: This soup is filling on its own, but you can certainly add 2 cups of uncooked short-cut pasta to the soup after the cooking cycle is complete and simmer using the "Sauté" mode until the pasta is tender.

Per Serving: Calories: 255; Protein: 18g; Fat: 11g; Saturated Fat: 3.5g; Carbohydrates: 19g; Sugar: 5.5g; Sodium: 294mg; Fiber: 3.5g

IRISH-INSPIRED LAMB STEW WITH STOUT

DAIRY-FREE, FREEZER-FRIENDLY

When you think of Ireland, you might think of lamb, potatoes, and stout beer. This recipe combines all those iconic flavors in stew form. Thick chunks of melt-in-your-mouth lamb and tender root vegetables are simmered in a rich, gravy-like broth. Serve it with some whole-grain bread with Irish butter to soak up every last bit of the sauce.

SERVES: 6

PREP TIME: 5 MINUTES

SAUTÉ TIME: 8 MINUTES

PRESSURIZATION TIME: 10 MINUTES

COOK TIME: 30 MINUTES ON "MANUAL" MODE UNDER HIGH PRESSURE

RELEASE: NATURAL RELEASE FOR 10 MINUTES, THEN QUICK RELEASE

TOTAL TIME: 1 HOUR 3 MINUTES

2 tablespoons olive oil

1½ pounds lamb shoulder, cut into 1-inch pieces

1 onion, diced

2 garlic cloves, minced

3 carrots, peeled and chopped

2 parsnips, peeled and chopped

2 Yukon Gold or red potatoes, skin left on and cut into 1-inch pieces

1 rosemary sprig

4 thyme sprigs

2 tablespoons tomato paste

1 (12-ounce) bottle dark stout beer

1 cup Roasted Beef Bone Stock (page 19) or store-bought unsalted beef broth

2 teaspoons cornstarch

¼ cup water

Salt

Freshly ground black pepper

Freshly chopped flat-leaf parsley, for garnish

1. Turn on the electric pressure cooker and select the "Sauté" mode. Heat the olive oil and cook the lamb for 5 minutes, or until browned. Add the onion and garlic and cook for 2 minutes, or until the onion is soft. Turn off the "Sauté" mode.

2. Add the carrots, parsnips, potatoes, rosemary, thyme, tomato paste, beer, and broth, and stir to combine.

3. Secure the lid. Select the "Manual" mode, and set the cooking time for 30 minutes under High Pressure. When the cooking cycle is complete, natural release for 10 minutes, then quick release any remaining steam.

4. In a separate bowl, whisk together the cornstarch and water. Select the "Sauté" mode again and bring the stew to a simmer. Then, add the cornstarch mixture and stir for 1 minute, or until the stew has thickened. Turn the electric pressure cooker off.

5. Season with salt and pepper to taste. Garnish with parsley before serving.

TIP: If you don't like the flavor of stout beer, you can substitute a lighter beer, such as pilsner or ale, or just use more beef broth.

Per Serving: Calories: 326; Protein: 22g; Fat: 12g; Saturated Fat: 4g; Carbohydrates: 28g; Sugar: 6g; Sodium: 155mg; Fiber: 4.5g

SPANISH-STYLE CHICKEN STEW

45 MINUTES OR LESS, DAIRY-FREE, FREEZER-FRIENDLY, GLUTEN-FREE

The Spanish-style stew packs a big flavor punch with tender, juicy chicken thighs drenched in a vibrant saffron broth. The addition of olives gives it a salty bite, and a sprinkle of almonds at the end provides a nice crunch. Your taste buds will thank you!

SERVES: 4

PREP TIME: 5 MINUTES

SAUTÉ TIME: 10 MINUTES

PRESSURIZATION TIME:
6 MINUTES

COOK TIME: 10 MINUTES ON "MANUAL" MODE UNDER HIGH PRESSURE

RELEASE: NATURAL RELEASE FOR 10 MINUTES, THEN QUICK RELEASE

TOTAL TIME: 41 MINUTES

2 tablespoons olive oil

2 pounds skinless, boneless chicken thighs

1 onion, diced

4 garlic cloves, minced

Pinch saffron threads

1 teaspoon paprika

1 cup pitted green olives, coarsely chopped

½ cup dry sherry or white wine

1 cup Chicken Broth (page 16) or store-bought unsalted chicken broth

Salt

Freshly ground black pepper

Chopped toasted almonds, for garnish

Freshly chopped flat-leaf parsley, for garnish

1. Turn on the electric pressure cooker and select the "Sauté" mode. Heat the olive oil and cook the chicken thighs, turning once, for 8 minutes, or until browned on both sides. Transfer the cooked chicken to a plate and set aside.

2. Add the onion and garlic and cook for 2 minutes, or until the onion is soft. Turn off the "Sauté" mode. Add the saffron, paprika, olives, sherry, broth, and cooked chicken thighs, and stir to combine.

3. Secure the lid. Select the "Manual" mode, and set the cooking time for 10 minutes under High Pressure. When the cooking cycle is complete, natural release for 10 minutes, then quick release any remaining steam.

4. Season with salt and pepper to taste. Garnish with almonds and parsley before serving.

TIP: This dish is best served with rice or bread, and perhaps a glass or two of refreshing, citrusy sangria. Simply pour a 750-ml bottle of white wine into a pitcher with ½ cup of brandy, one sliced orange, lemon, and lime, and sugar to taste. Let it chill for at least 6 hours and serve over ice with a splash of club soda.

Per Serving (without garnish): Calories: 424; Protein: 47g; Fat: 21g; Saturated Fat: 2.5g; Carbohydrates: 8g; Sugar: 1.5g; Sodium: 741mg; Fiber: 0.5g

CHICKEN POTPIE SOUP WITH PUFF PASTRY CROUTONS

When it's cold and gray out, a steaming hot bowl of this chicken potpie soup is the perfect antidote to the miserable weather. Even if it's warm and sunny where you are, your entire family will be sure to enjoy this quintessential comfort dish. It seems to taste twice as good with the flaky puff pastry croutons floating on top!

SERVES: 6

PREP TIME: 15 MINUTES

SAUTÉ TIME: 3 MINUTES

PRESSURIZATION TIME: 12 MINUTES

COOK TIME: 10 MINUTES ON "MANUAL" MODE UNDER HIGH PRESSURE

RELEASE: QUICK RELEASE

TOTAL TIME: 40 MINUTES

FOR THE PUFF PASTRY CROUTONS

All-purpose flour, for dusting

1 frozen puff pastry sheet, defrosted overnight in the refrigerator

2 tablespoons unsalted butter, melted

Salt

Freshly ground black pepper

FOR THE SOUP

1 onion, diced

2 garlic cloves, minced

2 carrots, peeled and diced

2 celery stalks, diced

½ teaspoon poultry seasoning

1 pound boneless, skinless chicken breast, cut into bite-size pieces

3 cups Chicken Broth (page 16) or store-bought unsalted chicken broth

2 tablespoons cornstarch

2 cups milk

1 cup frozen peas

Salt

Freshly ground black pepper

TO MAKE THE PUFF PASTRY CROUTONS

1. Preheat the oven to 400°F. Line a baking sheet with parchment paper. Lightly dust a work surface with flour.

2. Unroll the puff pastry sheet onto the floured surface and brush it with melted butter. Season with salt and pepper to taste. Use cookie cutters to cut the pastry into your desired shapes or cut it into squares. Place them on the prepared baking sheet.

3. Bake for 10 to 15 minutes, or until golden brown and flaky. Remove the croutons from oven and let them cool completely on baking sheet.

TO MAKE THE SOUP

4. Place the onion, garlic, carrots, celery, poultry seasoning, chicken breast, and broth in the inner pot of the pressure cooker.

5. Secure the lid. Select the "Manual" mode, and set the cooking time for 10 minutes under High Pressure. When the cooking cycle is complete, quick release any remaining steam.

6. In a separate bowl, whisk together the cornstarch and milk. Select the "Sauté" mode and bring the soup to a simmer. Then, add the cornstarch mixture and stir for 1 minute, or until the soup has thickened.

7. Stir in the peas and simmer for 2 minutes or until heated through. Turn the electric pressure cooker off.

8. Season with salt and pepper to taste. Serve with the puff pastry croutons.

Per Serving: Calories: 388; Protein: 27g; Fat: 18g; Saturated Fat: 9.5g; Carbohydrates: 35g; Sugar: 8.5g; Sodium: 311mg; Fiber: 3g

ZUPPA TOSCANA

Why eat soup out of a can when you can make something so much better? This hearty and creamy soup is full of sausage, potatoes, and kale, and the best part is that it's ready in about 30 minutes. If you're looking for a delectable soup with slow-simmered flavor, it doesn't get much better than this.

SERVES: 6

PREP TIME: 5 MINUTES

SAUTÉ TIME: 10 MINUTES

PRESSURIZATION TIME: 12 MINUTES

COOK TIME: 5 MINUTES ON "MANUAL" MODE UNDER HIGH PRESSURE

RELEASE: QUICK RELEASE

TOTAL TIME: 32 MINUTES

1 tablespoon olive oil

1 pound mild or spicy Italian sausage, casings removed

1 onion, diced

2 garlic cloves, minced

½ teaspoon Italian seasoning

3 russet potatoes, diced

6 cups Chicken Broth (page 16) or store-bought unsalted chicken broth

1 cup heavy (whipping) cream

3 cups lacinato or curly kale, trimmed and chopped

Salt

Freshly ground black pepper

Grated Parmesan, for serving

1. Turn on the electric pressure cooker and select the "Sauté" mode. Heat the olive oil and cook the sausage, breaking up large pieces into small crumbles, for 5 minutes, or until browned. Transfer the sausage to a plate lined with paper towels and set aside. Drain off excess grease, leaving about 1 tablespoon of fat in the pot.

2. Cook onion and garlic for 2 minutes, or until the onion is soft. Turn off the "Sauté" mode.

3. Add the Italian seasoning, potatoes, and broth, and stir to combine.

4. Secure the lid. Select the "Manual" mode, and set the cooking time for 5 minutes under High Pressure. When the cooking cycle is complete, quick release any remaining steam.

5. Select the "Sauté" mode again and bring the soup to a simmer. Stir in the cooked sausage, heavy cream, and kale and simmer for 3 minutes, or until the kale is wilted.

6. Season with salt and pepper to taste. Serve with the Parmesan.

TIP: For a low-carb version, substitute one head of cauliflower cut into florets for the potatoes.

Per Serving (without garnish): Calories: 381; Protein: 15g; Fat: 27g; Saturated Fat: 13g; Carbohydrates: 23g; Sugar: 4g; Sodium: 439mg; Fiber: 2g

LASAGNA SOUP

45 MINUTES OR LESS

Lasagna soup is one of the most popular dishes on my blog, so I decided to convert it into an electric pressure cooker version and never looked back. This recipe is easier to make than the original, without having to constantly stir the pot to ensure the lasagna noodles are fully submerged in the broth as they cook. This delicious weeknight staple is perfect for those days when you need to get dinner on the table quickly.

SERVES: 6

PREP TIME: 5 MINUTES

SAUTÉ TIME: 7 MINUTES

PRESSURIZATION TIME: 10 MINUTES

COOK TIME: 6 MINUTES ON "MANUAL" MODE UNDER HIGH PRESSURE

RELEASE: QUICK RELEASE

TOTAL TIME: 28 MINUTES

1 tablespoon olive oil

1 pound ground beef

1 onion, diced

3 garlic cloves, minced

1 teaspoon dried basil

1 teaspoon dried oregano

½ teaspoon dried thyme

¼ teaspoon red pepper flakes

2 tablespoons tomato paste

1 (28-ounce) can diced tomatoes

8 lasagna noodles, broken into bite-size pieces

4 cups Roasted Beef Bone Stock (page 19) or Chicken Stock (page 18) or store-bought unsalted beef or chicken broth

Salt

Freshly ground black pepper

1 cup ricotta cheese

1 cup shredded mozzarella

Grated Parmesan, for serving

1. Turn on the electric pressure cooker and select the "Sauté" mode. Heat the olive oil and cook the ground beef for 5 minutes, or until browned. Drain off excess grease, leaving about 1 tablespoon of oil in the pot.

2. Add the onion and garlic and cook for 2 minutes, or until the onion is soft. Turn off the "Sauté" mode.

3. Add the basil, oregano, thyme, red pepper flakes, tomato paste, diced tomatoes with their juices, lasagna noodles, and stock, and stir to combine.

4. Secure the lid. Select the "Manual" mode, and set the cooking time for 6 minutes under High Pressure. When the cooking cycle is complete, quick release any remaining steam.

5. Season with salt and pepper to taste.

6. In a bowl, mix together the ricotta and mozzarella. To serve, ladle soup into bowls, then top with heaping tablespoons of the cheese mixture. Sprinkle it with the Parmesan before serving.

TIP: You can replace the diced tomatoes and tomato paste with a 24-ounce jar of marinara sauce.

Per Serving (without garnish): Calories: 471; Protein: 31g; Fat: 20g; Saturated Fat: 8.5g; Carbohydrates: 40g; Sugar: 7.5g; Sodium: 560mg; Fiber: 3.5g

BEER CHEESE SOUP

This pub classic is for all the beer and cheese lovers out there. It's creamy, cheesy, buttery, and topped with bacon bits, popcorn, or homemade pretzel croutons for good measure (see Tip, page 147). How can you go wrong with that? The best part about this recipe is that you can have fun and switch it up with your favorite beer and cheese combination—pilsner and aged cheddar would taste amazing as well!

SERVES: 4

PREP TIME: 5 MINUTES

SAUTÉ TIME: 5 MINUTES

PRESSURIZATION TIME: 10 MINUTES

COOK TIME: 5 MINUTES ON "MANUAL" MODE UNDER HIGH PRESSURE

RELEASE: QUICK RELEASE

TOTAL TIME: 25 MINUTES

2 tablespoons unsalted butter

1 onion, diced

2 garlic cloves, minced

2 carrots, diced

1 celery stalk, diced

⅓ cup all-purpose flour

½ teaspoon dry mustard powder

⅛ teaspoon cayenne pepper

3 cups Chicken Broth (page 16) or store-bought unsalted chicken broth

1 (12-ounce) bottle beer

1 cup half-and-half

3 cups grated sharp cheddar

Salt

Freshly ground black pepper

2 tablespoons freshly chopped chives, for serving

1. Turn on the electric pressure cooker and select the "Sauté" mode. Melt the butter and cook the onion, garlic, carrots, and celery for 4 minutes, until the vegetables are soft. Add the flour and cook for 1 minute, or until the vegetables are well coated. Turn off the "Sauté" mode.

2. Add the mustard powder, cayenne pepper, broth, and beer, and stir to combine.

3. Secure the lid. Select the "Manual" mode, and set the cooking time for 5 minutes under High Pressure. When the cooking cycle is complete, quick release any remaining steam.

4. Using an immersion blender, traditional blender, or food processor, blend the soup until smooth.

5. Select the "Sauté" mode again and bring the soup to a simmer. Then, stir in the half-and-half and gradually stir in the cheddar until melted. Turn the electric pressure cooker off.

6. Season with salt and pepper to taste. Garnish with chives before serving.

TIP: Pretzel croutons are a delicious garnish for this soup. To make them, toss together two cubed soft pretzels, 2 tablespoons of melted unsalted butter, 1 teaspoon of Dijon mustard, and ½ teaspoon of hot sauce on a large baking sheet. Season with salt and pepper to taste. Bake at 350°F, stirring occasionally, for 10 to 15 minutes, or until toasted and golden brown. Remove the croutons from the oven and let them cool completely on the baking sheet before serving.

Per Serving: Calories: 590; Protein: 26g; Fat: 41g; Saturated Fat: 24g; Carbohydrates: 24g; Sugar: 6.5g; Sodium: 719mg; Fiber: 2g

PORK GREEN CHILI

DAIRY-FREE, FREEZER-FRIENDLY, GLUTEN-FREE

Pork green chili is possibly the unofficial state food of Colorado (sometimes called Colorado green chili). There are so many variations of this favorite, which is often served smothered over burritos, burgers, cheese fries, and hash. Make a full batch of this zesty, bright stew so you can enjoy it on its own for dinner one night and use it as a delicious topping to your next meal.

SERVES: 4

PREP TIME: 10 MINUTES

SAUTÉ TIME: 7 MINUTES

PRESSURIZATION TIME: 10 MINUTES

COOK TIME: 35 MINUTES ON "MANUAL" MODE UNDER HIGH PRESSURE

RELEASE: QUICK RELEASE

TOTAL TIME: 1 HOUR 2 MINUTES

2 tablespoons olive oil

1½ pounds boneless pork shoulder, cut into 1-inch pieces

1 onion, diced

3 garlic cloves, minced

½ pound fresh tomatillos, husks removed and diced

1 jalapeño pepper, seeded and diced

2 cups roasted Hatch green chiles, diced

½ cup packed cilantro, chopped, plus more for serving

1 teaspoon ground cumin

½ teaspoon ground coriander

½ teaspoon dried oregano

3 cups Chicken Broth (page 16) or store-bought unsalted chicken broth

Salt

Freshly ground black pepper

Lime wedges, serving

Tortilla chips, for serving

1. Turn on the electric pressure cooker and select the "Sauté" mode. Heat the olive oil and cook the pork for 5 minutes, or until browned. Add the onion and garlic and cook for 2 minutes, or until the onion is soft. Turn off the "Sauté" mode.

2. Add the tomatillos, jalapeño pepper, Hatch chiles, cilantro, cumin, coriander, oregano, and broth, and stir to combine.

3. Secure the lid. Select the "Manual" mode, and set the cooking time for 35 minutes under High Pressure. When the cooking cycle is complete, quick release any remaining steam.

4. Transfer 2 cups of the stew mixture (without pork) to a blender or food processor and blend until smooth. Return the blended mixture to the pot and stir in. Turn the electric pressure cooker off.

5. Season with salt and pepper to taste. Serve with cilantro, lime wedges, and tortilla chips.

TIP: If you have access to fresh Hatch chiles, you can roast them by placing them on a baking sheet under the broiler until the skin is blistered and slightly blackened. Transfer them to a bowl covered with plastic wrap for 10 minutes. Once they are cool enough to handle, peel away the skin and remove the seeds and stems before chopping them. If Hatch chiles are not available, you can substitute two (7-ounce) cans of diced green chiles.

Per Serving (without garnish): Calories: 345; Protein: 42g; Fat: 13g; Saturated Fat: 3g; Carbohydrates: 12g; Sugar: 4.5g; Sodium: 489mg; Fiber: 1.5g

RUSTIC ITALIAN-STYLE PORK RIB AND CHICKPEA SOUP

FREEZER-FRIENDLY, GLUTEN-FREE

This uncomplicated, rustic soup is made with simple ingredients, as are many of Italy's most delicious dishes. Don't let its simplicity fool you; it's amazingly comforting and has such great slow-cooked flavors. Pork ribs are not commonly used in soups, but they're perfect in this case as they essentially create a stock while the soup simmers away.

SERVES: 6

PREP TIME: 5 MINUTES

SAUTÉ TIME: 10 MINUTES

PRESSURIZATION TIME: 10 MINUTES

COOK TIME: 40 MINUTES ON "MANUAL" MODE UNDER HIGH PRESSURE

RELEASE: QUICK RELEASE

TOTAL TIME: 1 HOUR 5 MINUTES

2 tablespoons olive oil

1½ pounds pork spareribs, silverskin removed and cut between ribs

1 onion, diced

3 garlic cloves, minced

1 carrot, peeled and diced

1 celery stalk, diced

2 bay leaves

1 rosemary sprig

4 thyme sprigs

2 (15-ounce) cans chickpeas, rinsed and drained

3 cups Chicken Broth (page 16) or store-bought unsalted chicken broth

3 cups trimmed and chopped lacinato or curly kale

Salt

Freshly ground black pepper

Grated Parmesan, for serving

1. Turn on the electric pressure cooker and select the "Sauté" mode. Heat the olive oil and cook the spareribs for 5 minutes, or until browned. Remove and set aside.

2. Add the onion and garlic and cook for 2 minutes, or until the onion is soft. Turn off the "Sauté" mode.

3. Add the carrot, celery, bay leaves, rosemary, thyme, chickpeas, broth, and cooked spareribs, and stir to combine.

4. Secure the lid. Select the "Manual" mode, and set the cooking time for 40 minutes under High Pressure. When the cooking cycle is complete, quick release any remaining steam.

5. Remove and discard the rosemary and thyme sprigs.

6. Select the "Sauté" mode again and bring the soup to a simmer. Stir in the kale and let it simmer for 3 minutes, or until wilted. Turn the electric pressure cooker off.

7. Season with salt and pepper to taste. To serve, leave the ribs whole or remove the meat from the ribs and shred it with two forks. Sprinkle with the Parmesan.

TIP: If you prefer a thicker, stew-like consistency, after the cooking cycle is complete, transfer about 2 cups of the chickpeas and broth to a blender and puree until smooth before adding it back to the soup.

Per Serving (without garnish): Calories: 414; Protein: 24g; Fat: 21g; Saturated Fat: 6g; Carbohydrates: 33g; Sugar: 6.5g; Sodium: 387mg; Fiber: 8.5g

SPICY PORK AND MISO RAMEN

A huge upgrade from packaged instant ramen, this quick version of miso ramen is perfect for when cravings hit on a random weeknight and you just need a bowl of tasty noodles. When you serve this soup, be sure to customize it with a variety of toppings to call it your own.

SERVES: 4

PREP TIME: 10 MINUTES

SAUTÉ TIME: 6 MINUTES

PRESSURIZATION TIME: 12 MINUTES

COOK TIME: 10 MINUTES ON "MANUAL" MODE UNDER HIGH PRESSURE

RELEASE: QUICK RELEASE

TOTAL TIME: 38 MINUTES

10 ounces dried or fresh ramen noodles

1 tablespoon vegetable oil

8 ounces ground pork

1 shallot, diced

2 garlic cloves, minced

1 teaspoon freshly grated ginger

½ cup white miso

1½ teaspoons toasted sesame oil

1 tablespoon sugar

2 tablespoons chili bean sauce

6 cups Chicken Broth (page 16) or store-bought unsalted chicken broth

Salt

SUGGESTIONS FOR TOPPINGS
Soft-boiled eggs, corn, sliced bamboo shoots, bean sprouts, nori (seaweed), toasted sesame seeds, sliced scallions

1. Cook the noodles according to the package directions and rinse them with cold water. Drain well and set aside.

2. Turn on the electric pressure cooker and select the "Sauté" mode. Heat the vegetable oil and cook the pork for 4 minutes, or until browned. Add the shallot, garlic, and ginger and cook for 1 minute, or until shallot is soft. Turn off the "Sauté" mode.

3. Add the miso, sesame oil, sugar, chili bean sauce, and broth, and stir to combine.

4. Secure the lid. Select the "Manual" mode, and set the cooking time for 10 minutes under High Pressure. When the cooking cycle is complete, quick release any remaining steam.

5. Select the "Sauté" mode again. Add the cooked noodles, allow the soup to come to a simmer, and simmer for 1 minute, or until warmed through. Turn the electric pressure cooker off.

6. Season with salt to taste. Serve with your desired toppings.

TIP: Chili bean sauce (also known as *doubanjiang*) is a Chinese-style spicy fermented bean paste with red chile peppers. Substitutes for chili bean sauce include *sambal oelek* and chili garlic sauce.

To make soft-boiled eggs, bring a pot of water to a boil over medium-high heat, add the eggs to the water, cover them with a lid, and cook for 6 minutes. Remove the eggs, place them in an ice water bath, and peel the shells when they're cool enough to handle.

Per Serving (without toppings): Calories: 550; Protein: 22g; Fat: 20g; Saturated Fat: 5g; Carbohydrates: 70g; Sugar: 10g; Sodium: 1,549mg; Fiber: 2.5g

BEEF BOURGUIGNON

FREEZER-FRIENDLY

Inspired by a trip to the wine region of Burgundy, France, this soup is like a walk down memory lane. Even as we were savoring the namesake dish, I knew immediately that I wanted to go home and create an easier and quicker version that has exactly the same rich, deep, savory flavors. The result was these tender, fall-apart beef chunks simmered with earthy mushrooms, sweet pearl onions, and carrots in an irresistible red wine sauce.

SERVES: 6

PREP TIME: 5 MINUTES

SAUTÉ TIME: 16 MINUTES

PRESSURIZATION TIME: 6 MINUTES

COOK TIME: 40 MINUTES ON "MANUAL" MODE UNDER HIGH PRESSURE

RELEASE: QUICK RELEASE

TOTAL TIME: 1 HOUR 7 MINUTES

6 bacon slices, diced

2 pounds beef chuck, cut into 2-inch pieces

2 cups red wine

2 carrots, cut into 2-inch pieces

2 cups pearl onions, peeled

4 garlic cloves, minced

6 thyme sprigs

2 bay leaves

8 ounces white button mushrooms, quartered

2 tablespoons tomato paste

1½ cups Roasted Beef Bone Stock (page 19) or store-bought unsalted beef broth

2 tablespoons unsalted butter, softened

2 tablespoons all-purpose flour

Salt

Freshly ground black pepper

Freshly chopped flat-leaf parsley, for garnish

1. Turn on the electric pressure cooker and select the "Sauté" mode. Cook the bacon for 5 minutes, or until crisp. Retain about 1 tablespoon of fat in the pot. Transfer the bacon to a plate lined with paper towels and set aside.

2. Add the beef chuck and cook for 5 minutes, or until browned. Add the red wine and simmer for 5 minutes. Turn off the "Sauté" mode.

3. Add the carrots, onions, garlic, thyme, bay leaves, mushrooms, tomato paste, stock, and cooked bacon, and stir to combine.

4. Secure the lid. Select the "Manual" mode, and set the cooking time for 40 minutes under High Pressure. When the cooking cycle is complete, quick release any remaining steam.

5. Remove and discard the thyme and bay leaves.

6. In a separate bowl, combine the unsalted butter and flour. Select the "Sauté" mode again and bring the stew to a simmer. Then, add the butter mixture and stir for 1 minute, or until the stew has thickened. Turn the electric pressure cooker off.

7. Season with salt and pepper to taste. Garnish with parsley before serving.

TIP: Cook with a dry red wine like burgundy, cabernet sauvignon, or Chianti, but make sure you like the taste of the wine, as the flavors of the stew depend on it.

Per Serving: Calories: 406; Protein: 38g; Fat: 16g; Saturated Fat: 7g; Carbohydrates: 14g; Sugar: 3.5g; Sodium: 299mg; Fiber: 1.5g

OXTAIL AND CABBAGE SOUP

DAIRY-FREE, FREEZER-FRIENDLY, GLUTEN-FREE

They say taste triggers memories, and, for me, this soup certainly triggers the most comforting memories of my mom's cooking. Growing up, my mom always made this soup for our family, so whenever I feel homesick, I turn to this reliable recipe. I hope you love it as much as my family and I do.

SERVES: 6

PREP TIME: 5 MINUTES

SAUTÉ TIME: 4 MINUTES

PRESSURIZATION TIME: 10 MINUTES

COOK TIME: 1 HOUR ON "MANUAL" MODE UNDER HIGH PRESSURE

RELEASE: QUICK RELEASE

TOTAL TIME: 1 HOUR 19 MINUTES

---

2 tablespoons olive oil

3 pounds oxtail, rinsed and patted dry

1 onion, sliced

1 teaspoon dried thyme

2 bay leaves

2 tablespoons tomato paste

1 tablespoon Worcestershire sauce

4 cups Roasted Beef Bone Stock (page 19) or store-bought unsalted beef broth

1 Yukon Gold potato, diced

2 carrots, diced

1 celery stalk, diced

3 cups green cabbage, cut into 1-inch pieces

Salt

Freshly ground black pepper

Freshly chopped flat-leaf parsley, for garnish

1. Turn on the electric pressure cooker and select the "Sauté" mode. Heat the olive oil and cook the oxtail for 2 minutes per side, or until browned on both sides. Turn off the "Sauté" mode.

2. Add the onion, thyme, bay leaves, tomato paste, Worcestershire sauce, and stock, and stir to combine.

3. Secure the lid. Select the "Manual" mode, and set the cooking time for 45 minutes under High Pressure. When the cooking cycle is complete, quick release any remaining steam.

4. Open the lid and stir in the potato, carrots, celery, and cabbage. Secure the lid. Select the "Manual" mode again, and set the cooking time for 15 minutes under High Pressure. When the cooking cycle is complete, quick release any remaining steam.

5. Remove and discard the bay leaves. Turn the electric pressure cooker off.

6. Season with salt and pepper to taste. Garnish with parsley before serving.

TIP: Since oxtail consists of mainly bone and cartilage, it has naturally high gelatin content and needs to be cooked for quite a while. When shopping, look for equal-size pieces of oxtail so they cook up more evenly.

Per Serving: Calories: 396; Protein: 36g; Fat: 21g; Saturated Fat: 8g; Carbohydrates: 14g; Sugar: 4.5g; Sodium: 221mg; Fiber: 3g

UNSTUFFED PEPPER SOUP

I love taking classic recipes and giving them a little twist, like this unstuffed pepper soup. It's an easy way for you to enjoy the flavors of stuffed peppers with little fuss. And you'll get all the hearty flavor of a stuffed pepper—beef, vegetables, and rice—deconstructed into a delightful, nourishing soup!

SERVES: 6

PREP TIME: 5 MINUTES

SAUTÉ TIME: 7 MINUTES

PRESSURIZATION TIME: 10 MINUTES

COOK TIME: 5 MINUTES ON "MANUAL" MODE UNDER HIGH PRESSURE

RELEASE: NATURAL RELEASE FOR 10 MINUTES, THEN QUICK RELEASE

TOTAL TIME: 37 MINUTES

1 tablespoon olive oil

1 pound ground beef

1 onion, diced

2 garlic cloves, minced

1 celery stalk, diced

2 bell peppers, seeded and diced

½ teaspoon dried thyme

½ teaspoon dried oregano

1 teaspoon Italian seasoning

1 bay leaf

1 tablespoon Worcestershire sauce

1 (15-ounce) can tomato sauce

1 (15-ounce) can diced tomatoes

¾ cup uncooked long-grain white rice

4 cups Roasted Beef Bone Stock (page 19) or store-bought unsalted beef broth

Salt

Freshly ground black pepper

1. Turn on the electric pressure cooker and select the "Sauté" mode. Heat the olive oil and cook the ground beef for 5 minutes, or until browned. Drain off excess grease, leaving about 1 tablespoon of fat in the pot.

2. Add the onion and garlic and cook for 2 minutes, or until the onion is soft. Turn off the "Sauté" mode.

3. Add the celery, bell peppers, thyme, oregano, Italian seasoning, bay leaf, Worcestershire sauce, tomato sauce, diced tomatoes with their juices, rice, and stock, and stir to combine.

4. Secure the lid. Select the "Manual" mode, and set the cooking time for 5 minutes under High Pressure. When the cooking cycle is complete, natural release for 10 minutes, then quick release any remaining steam. Turn the electric pressure cooker off.

5. Season with salt and pepper to taste.

TIP: For a lighter version, try substituting ground turkey for the ground beef and use turkey or vegetable broth instead of the beef broth.

Per Serving: Calories: 316; Protein: 19g; Fat: 11g; Saturated Fat: 3.5g; Carbohydrates: 33g; Sugar: 8g; Sodium: 669mg; Fiber: 3g

VIETNAMESE-INSPIRED BEEF PHO

DAIRY-FREE

There are few broths with as much complexity, depth, and balance as an authentic, well-prepared pho. This recipe uses the automatic pressure cooker to simplify what might be a daylong process. Whenever I make this broth, I'll make a big batch and keep a few containers stashed in the freezer for emergencies. The extra roasting step is key, as the resulting depth of flavor makes it unquestionably worthwhile.

SERVES: 4

PREP TIME: 20 MINUTES

SAUTÉ TIME: 3 MINUTES

PRESSURIZATION TIME: 20 MINUTES

COOK TIME: 50 MINUTES ON "MANUAL" MODE UNDER HIGH PRESSURE

RELEASE: QUICK RELEASE

TOTAL TIME: 1 HOUR 33 MINUTES

3 pounds assorted beef bones, cut into smaller pieces

1 onion, quartered

1 (2-inch) piece fresh ginger, sliced

2 star anise

1 cinnamon stick

1 teaspoon coriander seeds

3 whole cloves

½ teaspoon black peppercorns

3 tablespoons fish sauce

1 tablespoon sugar

8 cups water

Salt

Freshly ground black pepper

1 pound dried flat rice noodles

½ pound beef sirloin steak

SUGGESTIONS FOR TOPPINGS
Cilantro, Thai basil, thinly sliced onions, bean sprouts, lime wedges, hoisin sauce, sriracha

1. Preheat the broiler and move the rack 3 inches from the heat source.

2. Arrange the bones, onion, and ginger on a rimmed baking sheet and place them under the broiler. Roast for 15 minutes, turning halfway through, until the bones are browned and onion is slightly charred.

3. Place the bones, onion, ginger, star anise, cinnamon, coriander, cloves, peppercorns, fish sauce, sugar, and water in the inner pot of the pressure cooker, making sure that the water is below the max line.

4. Secure the lid. Select the "Manual" mode, and set the cooking time for 50 minutes under High Pressure. When the cooking cycle is complete, quick release any remaining steam.

5. Pour the soup through a colander into a large heat-safe bowl, and discard the solids. Season the soup with salt and pepper to taste.

6. Meanwhile, cook the noodles according to the package directions and drain well. Slice the sirloin steak as thinly as possible.

7. Select the "Sauté" mode and bring the soup to a simmer. Then, stir in the steak slices and simmer for 3 minutes, or until cooked through. Turn the electric pressure cooker off.

8. To serve, divide the noodles among serving bowls and top them with the cooked beef slices and soup. Serve with your desired toppings.

TIP: Top choices for beef pho are sirloin steak, eye of round or London broil. To ensure that the beef gets cooked evenly, slice it as thinly as possible; placing it in the freezer for 15 minutes before slicing it helps firm the cut of meat so that you can slice it more thinly.

If you don't have time to make the beef broth from scratch, a quick way to make the pho broth is to use good-quality store-bought beef or bone broth, add the aromatics and spices, cook for 15 minutes under high pressure, and then quick release.

Per Serving (without garnish): Calories: 508; Protein: 25g; Fat: 3.5g; Saturated Fat: 0.5g; Carbohydrates: 95g; Sugar: 5g; Sodium: 938mg; Fiber: 0.5g

SMOKY CHIPOTLE BEEF BRISKET CHILI

FREEZER-FRIENDLY

Chili has become a staple for our family, and I've made dozens of batches over the years. If I had to include all my favorite flavors and components into the perfect bowl of chili, this would be the one. I know the addition of cocoa powder may sound a bit odd, but the bitterness of the cocoa will give this chili more depth and richness. If your mouth isn't watering yet, wait until you smell it!

SERVES: 6

PREP TIME: 5 MINUTES

SAUTÉ TIME: 15 MINUTES

PRESSURIZATION TIME:
10 MINUTES

COOK TIME: 1 HOUR ON "MANUAL" MODE UNDER HIGH PRESSURE

RELEASE: QUICK RELEASE

TOTAL TIME: 1 HOUR 30 MINUTES

4 bacon slices, diced

1½ pounds flat-cut beef brisket, cut into 1-inch pieces

1 onion, diced

4 garlic cloves, minced

2 tablespoons ancho chili powder

2 teaspoons ground cumin

1 teaspoon dried oregano

2 teaspoons unsweetened cocoa powder

1 bay leaf

1 chipotle pepper in adobo sauce, minced

1 (15-ounce) can diced fire-roasted tomatoes

1 (12-ounce) bottle Mexican-style beer

2 cups Roasted Beef Bone Stock (page 19) or store-bought unsalted beef broth

1 (15-ounce) can pinto beans, rinsed and drained

1 (15-ounce) can red kidney beans, rinsed and drained

Salt

Freshly ground black pepper

Sliced scallions, for serving

Shredded cheese, for serving

Tortilla chips, for serving

Sour cream, for serving

continued >

SMOKY CHIPOTLE BEEF BRISKET CHILI

continued

1. Turn on the electric pressure cooker and select the "Sauté" mode. Cook the bacon for 5 minutes, or until crisp. Retain about 1 tablespoon of fat in the pot. Transfer the bacon to a plate lined with paper towels and set aside.

2. Add the brisket and cook for 5 minutes, or until browned. Turn off the "Sauté" mode.

3. Add the onion, garlic, cooked bacon, chili powder, cumin, oregano, cocoa powder, bay leaf, chipotle pepper, diced tomatoes with their juices, beer, and stock, and stir to combine.

4. Secure the lid. Select the "Manual" mode, and set the cooking time for 1 hour under High Pressure. When the cooking cycle is complete, quick release any remaining steam.

5. Remove and discard the bay leaf.

6. Remove the brisket and shred it with two forks. Return the shredded meat to the chili.

7. Select the "Sauté" mode again and bring the chili to a simmer. Stir in the beans and simmer for 5 minutes, or until the beans are soft. Turn the electric pressure cooker off.

8. Season with salt and pepper to taste. Serve with scallions, shredded cheese, tortilla chips, and sour cream.

TIP: If you prefer, you can also make this recipe with beef chuck instead of beef brisket.

Per Serving (without garnish): Calories: 427; Protein: 36g; Fat: 15g; Saturated Fat: 5.5g; Carbohydrates: 33g; Sugar: 3.5g; Sodium: 777mg; Fiber: 9g

BEEF AND BARLEY SOUP

DAIRY-FREE, FREEZER-FRIENDLY

When you want to fill your home with a savory aroma that'll make everyone's mouth water, this beef and barley soup is an easy way to do it. I love that it's simple enough to make on a lazy Sunday afternoon and reheats well for a filling, nourishing meal throughout the week. This will keep well in your freezer so you can have a comforting, warm bowl on short notice.

SERVES: 6
PREP TIME: 5 MINUTES
SAUTÉ TIME: 7 MINUTES
PRESSURIZATION TIME:
12 MINUTES
COOK TIME: 25 MINUTES ON "MANUAL" MODE UNDER HIGH PRESSURE
RELEASE: QUICK RELEASE
TOTAL TIME: 49 MINUTES

2 tablespoons olive oil

1 pound beef chuck, cut into 1-inch pieces

1 onion, diced

4 garlic cloves, minced

2 carrots, diced

1 celery stalks, diced

8 ounces white button mushrooms, sliced

½ teaspoon dried thyme

2 bay leaves

1 tablespoon tomato paste

¾ cup uncooked pearled barley, rinsed and drained

6 cups Roasted Beef Bone Stock (page 19) or store-bought unsalted beef broth

Salt

Freshly ground black pepper

Freshly chopped flat-leaf parsley, for garnish

continued >

BEEF AND BARLEY SOUP

continued

1. Turn on the electric pressure cooker and select the "Sauté" mode. Heat the olive oil and cook the beef chuck for 5 minutes, or until browned. Add the onion and garlic and cook for 2 minutes, until the onion is soft. Turn off the "Sauté" mode.

2. Add the carrots, celery, mushrooms, thyme, bay leaves, tomato paste, barley, and stock, and stir to combine.

3. Secure the lid. Select the "Manual" mode, and set the cooking time for 25 minutes under High Pressure. When the cooking cycle is complete, quick release any remaining steam.

4. Remove and discard the bay leaves.

5. Season with salt and pepper to taste. Garnish with parsley before serving.

TIP: Many people will resort to using quick-cooking barley to save time. Since quick-cooking barley has been partially cooked and dried, it tends to fall apart during pressure cooking, so it's not the best substitute for this recipe.

Per Serving: Calories: 272; Protein: 22g; Fat: 8.5g; Saturated Fat: 2g; Carbohydrates: 27g; Sugar: 3g; Sodium: 169mg; Fiber: 5.5g

HUNGARIAN-STYLE GOULASH

FREEZER-FRIENDLY, GLUTEN-FREE

The first time I visited Hungary, I had my mind set on trying as many variations of goulash as I could. Some were thick like a stew; others had a consistency more like a soup. But there was one constant: the unmistakable flavor and color of paprika. Sweet Hungarian paprika is rather mild, so if you like the dish to be spicier, you can add some hot paprika. Serve this hearty dish with wide egg noodles or spaetzle tossed with butter and parsley for a tasty meal during the winter months.

SERVES: 6

PREP TIME: 5 MINUTES

SAUTÉ TIME: 8 MINUTES

PRESSURIZATION TIME: 10 MINUTES

COOK TIME: 30 MINUTES ON "MANUAL" MODE UNDER HIGH PRESSURE

RELEASE: QUICK RELEASE

TOTAL TIME: 53 MINUTES

2 tablespoons olive oil

2 pounds beef chuck, cut into 1-inch pieces

1 onion, diced

3 garlic cloves, minced

1 large red bell pepper, seeded and cut into 1-inch pieces

1 russet potato, diced

1 carrot, diced

2 tablespoons sweet Hungarian paprika

¼ teaspoon cayenne pepper

½ teaspoon caraway seeds

4 cups Roasted Beef Bone Stock (page 19) or store-bought unsalted beef broth

2 tablespoons cornstarch

¼ cup water

Salt

Freshly ground black pepper

Freshly chopped flat-leaf parsley, for serving

Sour cream, for serving

continued >

HUNGARIAN-STYLE GOULASH

continued

1. Turn on the electric pressure cooker and select the "Sauté" mode. Heat the olive oil and cook the beef chuck for 5 minutes, or until browned. Add the onion and garlic and cook for 2 minutes, or until the onion is soft. Turn off the "Sauté" mode.

2. Add the bell pepper, potato, carrot, paprika, cayenne pepper, caraway seeds, and stock, and stir to combine.

3. Secure the lid. Select the "Manual" mode, and set the cooking time for 30 minutes under High Pressure. When the cooking cycle is complete, quick release any remaining steam.

4. In a separate bowl, whisk together the cornstarch and water. Select the "Sauté" mode again and bring the soup to a simmer. Then, add the cornstarch mixture and stir for 1 minute, or until the soup has thickened. Turn the electric pressure cooker off.

5. Season with salt and pepper to taste. Serve with the parsley and sour cream.

TIP: If you don't care for the flavor of caraway seeds, simply omit them.

Per Serving (without garnish): Calories: 304; Protein: 36g; Fat: 12g; Saturated Fat: 3.5g; Carbohydrates: 14g; Sugar: 3g; Sodium: 181mg; Fiber: 2.5g

MEXICAN-STYLE ALBÓNDIGAS SOUP

DAIRY-FREE, FREEZER-FRIENDLY

Between the plump and tender meatballs, lightly spiced broth, and vegetables, there are so many delicious elements to this traditional Mexican-style soup that are sure to please everyone. It's filling and flavorful—the type of recipe you'd want to keep up your sleeve whenever you need a scrumptious, warming meal.

SERVES: 6

PREP TIME: 15 MINUTES

SAUTÉ TIME: 6 MINUTES

PRESSURIZATION TIME:
10 MINUTES

COOK TIME: 20 MINUTES ON "MANUAL" MODE UNDER HIGH PRESSURE

RELEASE: NATURAL RELEASE FOR 10 MINUTES, THEN QUICK RELEASE

TOTAL TIME: 1 HOUR 1 MINUTE

FOR THE MEATBALLS

1 pound ground beef or turkey

1 large egg

1 teaspoon salt

¼ teaspoon freshly ground black pepper

1 teaspoon garlic powder

½ teaspoon onion powder

1 teaspoon ground cumin

½ teaspoon dried oregano

2 tablespoons freshly chopped cilantro

¼ cup plain bread crumbs

¼ cup uncooked long-grain white rice

2 tablespoons olive oil

FOR THE SOUP

1 onion, diced

3 garlic cloves, minced

1 carrot, diced

1 celery stalk, diced

1 russet potato, cubed

2 teaspoons adobo sauce

1 (15-ounce) can diced tomatoes

4 cups Roasted Beef Bone Stock (page 19) or store-bought unsalted beef or turkey broth

Salt

Freshly ground black pepper

continued >

MEXICAN-STYLE ALBÓNDIGAS SOUP

continued

TO MAKE THE MEATBALLS

1. Mix together the ground beef, egg, salt, pepper, garlic powder, onion powder, cumin, oregano, cilantro, bread crumbs, and rice in a large bowl. Shape mixture into small (1-inch) meatballs.

2. Turn on the electric pressure cooker and select the "Sauté" mode. Heat the olive oil and cook the meatballs for 3 minutes per side, or until browned. Transfer the meatballs to a plate and set aside. Turn off the "Sauté" mode.

TO MAKE THE SOUP

3. Place the onion, garlic, carrot, celery, potato, adobo sauce, diced tomatoes with their juices, and stock in the inner pot of the pressure cooker, and stir to combine. Carefully add the meatballs to the soup.

4. Secure the lid. Select the "Manual" mode, and set the cooking time for 20 minutes under High Pressure. When the cooking cycle is complete, natural release for 10 minutes, then quick release any remaining steam. Turn the electric pressure cooker off.

5. Season with salt and pepper to taste.

TIP: Ground beef with a higher fat content (ideally 80 percent lean ground beef) produces the most flavorful and tender meatballs. But if you find that there's a lot of excess fat on your soup, you may skim it off with a slotted spoon before serving.

Per Serving: Calories: 319; Protein: 20g; Fat: 17g; Saturated Fat: 5.5g; Carbohydrates: 22g; Sugar: 3.5g; Sodium: 706mg; Fiber: 2.5g

OAXACAN-INSPIRED BARBACOA SOUP

FREEZER-FRIENDLY, GLUTEN-FREE

Traditionally made with lamb, this soup is meaty and hearty with a finishing zip and a hint of heat that is hard to beat. If you've never used these dried chiles before, you'll love the smoky, fruity flavor they provide without much heat. Some dishes actually do taste better the next day once the flavors have a chance to mingle and deepen, and this is one of them.

SERVES: 6

PREP TIME: 15 MINUTES

SAUTÉ TIME: 5 MINUTES

PRESSURIZATION TIME: 10 MINUTES

COOK TIME: 40 MINUTES ON "MANUAL" MODE UNDER HIGH PRESSURE

RELEASE: NATURAL RELEASE FOR 10 MINUTES, THEN QUICK RELEASE

TOTAL TIME: 1 HOUR 20 MINUTES

5 dried guajillo or pasilla chiles

2 dried ancho chiles

2 plum tomatoes, seeded and coarsely chopped

1 onion, coarsely chopped

4 garlic cloves, smashed

1 (4-ounce) can diced green chiles

2 tablespoons olive oil

2 pounds boneless lamb shoulder or beef chuck, cut into 2-inch pieces

1 tablespoon chili powder

1 teaspoon ground cumin

1 teaspoon dried oregano

½ teaspoon ground coriander

1 cinnamon stick

2 bay leaves

½ cup orange juice

4 cups Roasted Beef Bone Stock (page 19) or store-bought unsalted beef broth

Salt

Freshly ground black pepper

Corn tortillas, for serving

Diced white onions, for serving

Freshly chopped cilantro, for serving

Queso fresco, for serving

continued >

OAXACAN-INSPIRED BARBACOA SOUP

continued

1. Heat a skillet over high heat and toast the guajillo and ancho chiles for about 30 seconds per side, until they become fragrant.

2. Using kitchen scissors, remove the stems, seeds, and veins from the chiles and let them soak in a bowl of hot water for 10 minutes. Reserve ½ cup of the soaking liquid.

3. Place the rehydrated chiles in a blender or food processor with the tomatoes, onion, garlic, green chiles, and the reserved soaking liquid. Puree until smooth, adding more water as needed.

4. Turn on the electric pressure cooker and select the "Sauté" mode. Heat the olive oil and cook the lamb for 5 minutes, or until browned. Turn off the "Sauté" mode.

5. Add the chile mixture, chili powder, cumin, oregano, coriander, cinnamon, bay leaves, orange juice, and stock, and stir to combine.

6. Secure the lid. Select the "Manual" mode, and set the cooking time for 40 minutes under High Pressure. When the cooking cycle is complete, natural release for 10 minutes, then quick release any remaining steam.

7. Remove and discard the bay leaves.

8. Remove the lamb and shred it with two forks. Return the shredded meat to the soup. Turn the electric pressure cooker off.

9. Season with salt and pepper to taste. Serve with the tortillas, onions, cilantro, and queso fresco.

TIP: Use the leftover meat and soup as a filling for enchiladas, tacos, and burritos.

Per Serving (without garnish): Calories: 343; Protein: 33g; Fat: 17g; Saturated Fat: 6g; Carbohydrates: 12g; Sugar: 1.5g; Sodium: 237mg; Fiber: 2g

CHAPTER 7

SEAFOOD SOUPS

Seafood soups hold a special place in my heart; they were among the first dishes I experimented with when I started using the electric pressure cooker. The first time I made shellfish stock in it, I was amazed at how quickly it came together, with the extra perk of not having the fishy smell permeating every room of the house! In fact, the stock turned out to be even richer and more flavorful due to the lack of evaporation.

Rustic, comforting stews like Low-Country Shrimp Boil Soup (page 186) and Cod and Potato Stew (page 201), as well as refined soups like Classic French-Style Bouillabaisse (page 178) and Lobster Bisque (page 188) can be cooked in the electric pressure cooker with little hands-on time, as the pressure cooking quickly infuses the flavors of the vegetables, aromatics, and spices into the soup base. Since most seafood can easily get overcooked and become tough or rubbery, most of these recipes will call for adding the seafood at the end for a brief simmer to ensure a tender and moist texture. And for that reason, you can prepare the broth a day or two in advance (up to the point of adding the seafood) and finish it when it's serving time, which is ideal for those who meal prep or have guests over for dinner.

For the recipes in this section, it's best to use fish stock or shellfish stock as the base, as they will intensify the flavor of the soups. However, bottled clam juice also packs a ton of briny flavor, and Chicken Broth (page 16) or Vegetable Broth (page 14) can usually be used with good results.

< Lobster and Corn Chowder, page 207

CIOPPINO

No trip to San Francisco would be complete without a bowl of cioppino, a signature seafood stew that first became popular on Fisherman's Wharf, where Italian American fishermen would share their catches of the day and add to the communal stew. It's meant to be a versatile dish, so you can be creative with this recipe and use any kind of seafood you prefer. Squid, lump crabmeat, shucked oysters, and lobster are some of my favorite additions. Be sure to serve it with some sourdough bread for sopping up that delicious broth!

SERVES: 4

PREP TIME: 5 MINUTES

SAUTÉ TIME: 13 MINUTES

PRESSURIZATION TIME: 10 MINUTES

COOK TIME: 10 MINUTES ON "MANUAL" MODE UNDER HIGH PRESSURE

RELEASE: QUICK RELEASE

TOTAL TIME: 38 MINUTES

2 tablespoons olive oil

1 fennel bulb, fronds removed and diced

1 onion, diced

4 garlic cloves, minced

½ teaspoon red pepper flakes

½ teaspoon dried oregano

1 bay leaf

2 tablespoons tomato paste

1 (28-ounce) can diced tomatoes

1 cup dry white wine

3 cups Fish Stock (page 21) or Shellfish Stock (page 20) or store-bought unsalted fish or shellfish stock

1 pound littleneck clams and/or mussels, scrubbed

8 ounces sea or bay scallops

8 ounces large shrimp, peeled and deveined

1 pound halibut or other firm whitefish, cut into 2-inch pieces

Salt

Freshly ground black pepper

Freshly chopped flat-leaf parsley, for garnish

1. Turn on the electric pressure cooker and select the "Sauté" mode. Heat the olive oil and cook the fennel, onion, and garlic for 3 minutes, or until the vegetables start to become soft. Turn off the "Sauté" mode.

2. Add the red pepper flakes, oregano, bay leaf, tomato paste, diced tomatoes with their juices, wine, and stock, and stir to combine.

3. Secure the lid. Select the "Manual" mode, and set the cooking time for 10 minutes under High Pressure. When the cooking cycle is complete, quick release any remaining steam.

4. Remove and discard the bay leaf.

5. Select the "Sauté" mode again and bring the stew to a simmer. Then, add the clams, cover with a glass lid (or regular lid, but do not lock it in place), and simmer for 5 minutes, or until they open.

6. Add the scallops, shrimp, and halibut and simmer for 5 minutes or until just cooked through. Turn the electric pressure cooker off.

7. Season with salt and pepper to taste. Garnish with parsley before serving.

TIP: Sourdough herb crostini are a delicious garnish for this soup. To make them, cut a loaf of sourdough bread into 1-inch slices and brush them with 2 tablespoons of extra-virgin olive oil. Sprinkle with 1 teaspoon of herbes de Provence or Italian seasoning, salt, and freshly ground black pepper to taste. Place on a baking sheet and bake at 350°F for 10 minutes, or until golden brown. Remove the crostini from oven and let them cool completely on the baking sheet before serving.

Per Serving: Calories: 437; Protein: 50g; Fat: 9.5g; Saturated Fat: 1.5g; Carbohydrates: 25g; Sugar: 12g; Sodium: 710mg; Fiber: 5g

CLASSIC FRENCH-STYLE BOUILLABAISSE

`45 MINUTES OR LESS, DAIRY-FREE`

Brimming with seafood in an aromatic saffron broth, one bite of this Provençal seafood stew will transport you to the glistening blue seas and warm breezes of the Mediterranean coast. A variety of seafood can be used in this stew, but your best bet is simply using the freshest seafood you can find.

SERVES: 4

PREP TIME: 5 MINUTES

SAUTÉ TIME: 8 MINUTES

PRESSURIZATION TIME: 10 MINUTES

COOK TIME: 10 MINUTES ON "MANUAL" MODE UNDER HIGH PRESSURE

RELEASE: QUICK RELEASE

TOTAL TIME: 33 MINUTES

2 tablespoons olive oil

1 fennel bulb, fronds removed and diced

1 leek (white and light green parts only), thinly sliced

1 onion, diced

4 garlic cloves, minced

Pinch saffron threads

1 bay leaf

2 tablespoons pastis (optional)

2 plum tomatoes, seeded and coarsely chopped

2 Yukon Gold potatoes, skin left on and cut into 1-inch pieces

4 cups Fish Stock (page 21) or Shellfish Stock (page 20) or store-bought unsalted fish or shellfish stock

1 pound large shrimp, peeled and deveined

1 pound firm whitefish (like cod or red snapper), cut into 2-inch pieces

1 pound lobster tails, halved lengthwise through shell

Salt

Freshly ground black pepper

Toasted bread, for serving

1. Turn on the electric pressure cooker and select the "Sauté" mode. Heat the olive oil and cook the fennel, leek, onion, and garlic for 3 minutes, or until the vegetables start to become soft. Turn off the "Sauté" mode.

2. Add the saffron, bay leaf, pastis (if using), tomatoes, potatoes, and stock, and stir to combine.

3. Secure the lid. Select the "Manual" mode, and set the cooking time for 10 minutes under High Pressure. When the cooking cycle is complete, quick release any remaining steam.

4. Remove and discard the bay leaf.

5. Select the "Sauté" mode again and bring the stew to a simmer. Once the stew comes to a simmer, add the shrimp, whitefish, and lobster tails, and simmer for 5 to 7 minutes, or until just cooked through. Turn the electric pressure cooker off.

6. Season with salt and pepper to taste. Serve with toasted bread.

TIP: Pastis, an anise-flavored liqueur, is optional in this recipe, but it enhances the licorice flavor of the fennel nicely. Popular brands include Pernod and Ricard. If you can't find pastis, Greek ouzo would be a good substitute.

Per Serving (without bread): Calories: 499; Protein: 65g; Fat: 9.5g; Saturated Fat: 1.5g; Carbohydrates: 35g; Sugar: 11g; Sodium: 878mg; Fiber: 5.5g

THAI-INSPIRED TOM YUM SEAFOOD SOUP

45 MINUTES OR LESS, DAIRY-FREE, GLUTEN-FREE

My husband and I love Thai food. Whenever we visit Thailand, we indulge in dishes like green papaya salad and basil chicken to our hearts' content. But there's nothing like a steaming bowl of *tom yum goong* to truly stimulate our taste buds; it's spicy, sour, herbaceous, and never bland. Ever since our Thai friend taught us her family recipe, I've adapted it to the electric pressure cooker so it can be made quickly and easily.

SERVES: 6

PREP TIME: 5 MINUTES

SAUTÉ TIME: 5 MINUTES

PRESSURIZATION TIME: 12 MINUTES

COOK TIME: 8 MINUTES ON "MANUAL" MODE UNDER HIGH PRESSURE

RELEASE: QUICK RELEASE

TOTAL TIME: 30 MINUTES

2 shallots, sliced

2 lemongrass stalks (yellow part only), cut into 2-inch sections

1 (1-inch) piece galangal root, sliced

5 kaffir lime leaves

1 small bunch cilantro roots and stems

1 tablespoon Thai chili paste (*nam prik pao*)

2 tablespoons fish sauce

1 teaspoon brown sugar

2 tablespoons fresh lime juice

6 cups Shellfish Stock (page 20) or Vegetable Broth (page 14) or store-bought unsalted shellfish stock or vegetable broth

1 cup straw or white button mushrooms, sliced

3 cups mixed seafood (such as shrimp, calamari, scallops)

Salt

Freshly chopped cilantro, for garnish

Lime wedges, for garnish

1. Place the shallots, lemongrass, galangal root, lime leaves, cilantro roots and stems, chili paste, fish sauce, brown sugar, lime juice, and stock in the inner pot of the pressure cooker.

2. Secure the lid. Turn on the electric pressure cooker, select the "Manual" mode, and set the cooking time for 8 minutes under High Pressure. When the cooking cycle is complete, quick release any remaining steam.

3. Remove and discard the lemongrass stalks, galangal root, lime leaves, and cilantro roots and stems.

4. Select the "Sauté" mode and bring the soup to a simmer. Then, add the mushrooms and mixed seafood and simmer for 5 minutes, or until the seafood is cooked through. Turn the electric pressure cooker off.

5. Season with salt to taste. Garnish with cilantro and lime wedges before serving.

TIP: *Nam prik pao* is a Thai chili paste often made with ground chiles, garlic, shrimp paste, and tamarind. It can range from sweet and mild to pungent and fiery hot. If you're not sure about your desired heat level, add it at the end of cooking and adjust the amount according to your taste. Substitutes for *nam prik pao* include *sambal oelek*, sriracha, and chili garlic sauce.

Per Serving: Calories: 129; Protein: 20g; Fat: 1g; Saturated Fat: 0g; Carbohydrates: 10g; Sugar: 4g; Sodium: 744mg; Fiber: 1g

SMOKED SAUSAGE AND SEAFOOD GUMBO

45 MINUTES OR LESS, DAIRY-FREE, FREEZER-FRIENDLY

Gumbo is a Southern staple, and this recipe follows the cardinal rule of great gumbo making: cooking flour and oil until a rich brown roux forms. An authentic gumbo always includes the "holy trinity" of onions, bell peppers, and celery, as well as okra to create a stew-like consistency. If you're not a fan of okra, feel free to leave it out; the gumbo will still be tasty and soul satisfying.

SERVES: 4

PREP TIME: 5 MINUTES

SAUTÉ TIME: 20 MINUTES

PRESSURIZATION TIME: 10 MINUTES

COOK TIME: 10 MINUTES ON "MANUAL" MODE UNDER HIGH PRESSURE

RELEASE: QUICK RELEASE

TOTAL TIME: 45 MINUTES

⅓ cup vegetable oil

⅓ cup all-purpose flour

1 onion, diced

3 garlic cloves, minced

1 green bell pepper, seeded and diced

2 celery stalks, diced

2 bay leaves

1 tablespoon salt-free Cajun seasoning

12 ounces smoked andouille sausage, sliced

1 (15-ounce) can no-salt-added diced tomatoes

1 cup fresh or frozen okra, sliced

4 cups Chicken Broth (page 16) or store-bought unsalted chicken broth

8 ounces lump crabmeat

8 ounces large shrimp, peeled and deveined

Salt

Freshly ground black pepper

Cooked white rice, for serving

Sliced scallions, for serving

Hot sauce, for serving

1. Turn on the electric pressure cooker and select the "Sauté" mode. Heat the vegetable oil and cook the flour for 10 minutes, or until the roux is a brown color.

2. Add the onion, garlic, bell pepper, and celery and cook for 5 minutes, or until the vegetables start to become soft. Turn off the "Sauté" mode.

3. Add the bay leaves, Cajun seasoning, sausage, diced tomatoes with their juices, okra, and broth, and stir to combine.

4. Secure the lid. Select the "Manual" mode, and set the cooking time for 10 minutes under High Pressure. When the cooking cycle is complete, quick release any remaining steam.

5. Remove and discard the bay leaves.

6. Select the "Sauté" mode again and bring the soup to a simmer. Then, add the crabmeat and shrimp and simmer for 5 to 7 minutes, until cooked through. Turn the electric pressure cooker off.

7. Season with salt and pepper to taste. Serve with the rice, scallions, and hot sauce.

TIP: A good roux provides the gumbo with a rich, nutty flavor, but it requires some time and patience. Use the low setting on "Sauté" mode and stir the roux constantly with a spatula to prevent burning. If the low setting is not available in your model, start with the Normal setting on "Sauté" mode and, once the oil and flour start sizzling, switch to the "Keep Warm" mode. As far as the color of roux goes, some cooks say it should be the color of peanut butter, while others say the color of chocolate. If you have the time, darker (but not burnt) is always better.

Per Serving (without rice): Calories: 534; Protein: 41g; Fat: 30g; Saturated Fat: 6.5g; Carbohydrates: 26g; Sugar: 8.5g; Sodium: 1,181mg; Fiber: 5g

CHIPOTLE SHRIMP AND TOMATILLO SOUP

45 MINUTES OR LESS, DAIRY-FREE, FREEZER-FRIENDLY, GLUTEN-FREE

I love cooking with shrimp; its mild flavor lends itself to any number of possible seasonings and sauces. This soup has the best of both worlds—the fresh tartness of tomatillos and the smokiness of chipotle peppers in adobo sauce—providing depth and vibrant flavors without overpowering the succulent shrimp. Finished off with fresh cilantro and lime juice, it's a great soup for enjoying in the summer on the deck.

SERVES: 4

PREP TIME: 13 MINUTES

SAUTÉ TIME: 3 MINUTES

PRESSURIZATION TIME: 10 MINUTES

COOK TIME: 10 MINUTES ON "MANUAL" MODE UNDER HIGH PRESSURE

RELEASE: QUICK RELEASE

TOTAL TIME: 36 MINUTES

1 onion, quartered

3 garlic cloves, minced

1 pound fresh tomatillos, husks removed and coarsely chopped

1 chipotle pepper in adobo sauce, minced

½ teaspoon ground cumin

4 cups Shellfish Stock (page 20) or Vegetable Broth (page 14) or store-bought unsalted shrimp stock or vegetable broth, divided

1 (15-ounce) can hominy, rinsed and drained

1 pound large shrimp, peeled and deveined

Salt

Freshly ground black pepper

Freshly chopped cilantro, for garnish

Lime wedges, for garnish

1. In a blender, place the onion, garlic, tomatillos, chipotle pepper, cumin, and 2 cups of the stock and blend until smooth.

2. Add the tomatillo mixture, the remaining 2 cups of stock, and the hominy to the inner pot of the pressure cooker.

3. Secure the lid. Turn on the electric pressure cooker, select the "Manual" mode, and set the cooking time for 10 minutes under High Pressure. When the cooking cycle is complete, quick release any remaining steam.

4. Select the "Sauté" mode and bring the soup to a simmer. Then, add the shrimp and simmer for 3 to 5 minutes, or until cooked through. Turn the electric pressure cooker off.

5. Season with salt and pepper to taste. Garnish with cilantro and lime wedges before serving.

TIP: Since the shrimp is added to the soup in the last few minutes of cooking, there is minimal flavor extracted from them in that time frame. Therefore, making a shrimp stock from the shells helps extract as much flavor as possible and is really worth the effort in this recipe.

Per Serving: Calories: 198; Protein: 23g; Fat: 2.5g; Saturated Fat: 0.5g; Carbohydrates: 23g; Sugar: 8g; Sodium: 389mg; Fiber: 5g

LOW-COUNTRY SHRIMP BOIL SOUP

Inspired by the Low-Country shrimp boil, this soup will remind you of summer gatherings around large pots of shrimp and crawfish boiled with potatoes, smoked sausage, and corn on the cob, served on a newspaper-covered picnic table. It's a no-fuss, less-messy way to enjoy the dish, preferably with a bucket of ice-cold beer. I used Old Bay seasoning here, but it's equally delicious with Cajun seasoning.

SERVES: 4

PREP TIME: 5 MINUTES

SAUTÉ TIME: 7 MINUTES

PRESSURIZATION TIME: 10 MINUTES

COOK TIME: 7 MINUTES ON "MANUAL" MODE UNDER HIGH PRESSURE

RELEASE: QUICK RELEASE

TOTAL TIME: 29 MINUTES

2 tablespoons unsalted butter

1 onion, diced

1 green bell pepper, seeded and diced

3 garlic cloves, minced

2½ teaspoons Old Bay seasoning

12 ounces kielbasa sausage, sliced

12 ounces baby red potatoes, halved

1 cup fresh or frozen corn kernels

4 cups Chicken Broth (page 16) or Vegetable Broth (page 14) or store-bought unsalted chicken or vegetable broth

1 pound large shrimp, peeled and deveined

Salt

Freshly ground black pepper

Freshly chopped flat-leaf parsley, for garnish

Lemon wedges, for garnish

1. Turn on the electric pressure cooker and select the "Sauté" mode. Add the butter and cook the onion, bell pepper, and garlic for 4 minutes, or until the vegetables are soft. Turn off the "Sauté" mode.

2. Add the Old Bay seasoning, sausage, potatoes, corn, and broth, and stir to combine.

3. Secure the lid. Select the "Manual" mode, and set the cooking time for 7 minutes under High Pressure. When the cooking cycle is complete, quick release any remaining steam.

4. Select the "Sauté" mode again and bring the soup to a simmer. Then, add the shrimp and simmer for 3 to 5 minutes, or until cooked through. Turn the electric pressure cooker off.

5. Season with salt and pepper to taste. Garnish with parsley and lemon wedges before serving.

TIP: As a variation, substitute crawfish tail meat for the shrimp.

Per Serving: Calories: 448; Protein: 40g; Fat: 22g; Saturated Fat: 10g; Carbohydrates: 27g; Sugar: 6.5g; Sodium: 935mg; Fiber: 3g

LOBSTER BISQUE

Lobster is always a treat, and this bisque is a great way to enjoy it if you want something different from the standard steamed lobster and drawn butter. Using rice as a thickener is not common these days, but I learned this method in an old cookbook years ago and love the creamy texture it creates. Serve this classic lobster soup whenever you want to impress someone. It requires a bit of work, but it will make a showstopping dish, as the flavor and texture are up to par with anything you'd find at a fancy bistro.

SERVES: 4

PREP TIME: 5 MINUTES

SAUTÉ TIME: 2 MINUTES

PRESSURIZATION TIME:
12 MINUTES

COOK TIME: 10 MINUTES ON "MANUAL" MODE UNDER HIGH PRESSURE

RELEASE: QUICK RELEASE

TOTAL TIME: 29 MINUTES

6 cups lobster stock

1 tablespoon unsalted butter

3 shallots, diced

1 carrot, peeled and diced

1 celery stalk, diced

1/3 cup uncooked long-grain white rice

2 tablespoons tomato paste

1/8 teaspoon cayenne pepper

2 cups diced cooked lobster meat

1/2 cup heavy (whipping) cream

2 tablespoons fresh lemon juice

Salt

Freshly ground black pepper

1. Prepare the stock according to the recipe for Shellfish Stock (page 20), using the shells from steamed whole lobsters or lobster tails. Reserve the lobster meat.

2. Turn on the electric pressure cooker and select the "Sauté" mode. Melt the butter and cook the shallots for 1 minute, or until they are soft. Turn off the "Sauté" mode.

3. Add the carrot, celery, rice, tomato paste, cayenne pepper, and stock, and stir to combine.

4. Secure the lid. Select the "Manual" mode, and set the cooking time for 10 minutes under High Pressure. When the cooking cycle is complete, quick release any remaining steam.

5. Using an immersion blender, traditional blender, or food processor, blend the soup until smooth.

6. Select the "Sauté" mode again and bring the soup to a simmer. Then, stir in the lobster meat, heavy cream, and lemon juice, and simmer for 1 minute, or until heated through. Turn the electric pressure cooker off.

7. Season with salt and pepper to taste.

TIP: Instead of using lobster, you can substitute shrimp to make a more affordable yet equally tasty and decadent shrimp bisque.

Per Serving: Calories: 329; Protein: 22g; Fat: 15g; Saturated Fat: 9g; Carbohydrates: 29g; Sugar: 8g; Sodium: 402mg; Fiber: 3.5g

MUSSELS IN TOMATO-FENNEL BROTH

Get your napkins ready, because there's nothing like a big pot of mussels floating in a flavorful tomato and fennel broth. It's fresh, light, and simple at its best. If you want a little spicy kick, feel free to add a pinch of red pepper flakes to the broth. Other than some warm toasted bread (or French fries if you want to go the *moules frites* route) for dunking, you'll need nothing else with this dish.

SERVES: 4

PREP TIME: 5 MINUTES

SAUTÉ TIME: 8 MINUTES

PRESSURIZATION TIME:
5 MINUTES

COOK TIME: 10 MINUTES ON "MANUAL" MODE UNDER HIGH PRESSURE

RELEASE: QUICK RELEASE

TOTAL TIME: 28 MINUTES

2 tablespoons olive oil

1 fennel bulb, fronds removed and thinly sliced

2 shallots, sliced

2 garlic cloves, minced

½ cup dry white wine

1 pint cherry tomatoes, halved

4 thyme sprigs

½ cup Fish Stock (page 21) or store-bought unsalted fish stock or clam juice

3 pounds mussels, scrubbed

Salt

Freshly ground black pepper

Freshly chopped flat-leaf parsley, for serving

Lemon wedges, for serving

Crusty bread, for serving

1. Turn on the electric pressure cooker and select the "Sauté" mode. Heat the olive oil and cook the fennel, shallots, and garlic for 3 minutes, or until the vegetables start to become soft. Turn off the "Sauté" mode.

2. Add the wine, tomatoes, thyme, and stock, and stir to combine.

3. Secure the lid. Select the "Manual" mode, and set the cooking time for 10 minutes under High Pressure. When the cooking cycle is complete, quick release any remaining steam.

4. Remove and discard the thyme sprigs.

5. Select the "Sauté" mode again and bring the broth to a simmer. Then, add the mussels, cover with a glass lid (or regular lid, but do not lock it in place), and simmer for 5 minutes, or until they open. Turn the electric pressure cooker off.

6. Season with salt and pepper to taste. Serve with the parsley, lemon wedges, and plenty of crusty bread.

TIP: To clean the mussels, scrub them really well with a brush to remove any sand or debris on the shell, then soak them in a bowl of fresh water for about 15 minutes. Rinse and soak them again until there is no more sediment at the bottom of the bowl.

Per Serving (without bread): Calories: 422; Protein: 43g; Fat: 15g; Saturated Fat: 2.5g; Carbohydrates: 23g; Sugar: 4.5g; Sodium: 1,017mg; Fiber: 3g

MANHATTAN-STYLE CLAM CHOWDER

When I was growing up in New York, Randazzo's Clam Bar in Brooklyn was an institution. I still have fond memories of their zesty and flavorful Manhattan-Style Clam Chowder. Here's my take on the tomato-based clam chowder, which I feel rivals its thick, cream-based New England cousin any day. I use both chopped and whole clams for different textures and even sneak in a touch of heavy cream at the end to give the soup some richness.

SERVES: 4

PREP TIME: 5 MINUTES

SAUTÉ TIME: 7 MINUTES

PRESSURIZATION TIME: 10 MINUTES

COOK TIME: 7 MINUTES ON "MANUAL" MODE UNDER HIGH PRESSURE

RELEASE: QUICK RELEASE

TOTAL TIME: 29 MINUTES

4 bacon slices, diced

1 onion, diced

2 garlic cloves, minced

1 bay leaf

½ teaspoon dried thyme

¼ teaspoon celery seed

¼ teaspoon red pepper flakes

1 carrot, diced

2 celery stalks, diced

2 Yukon Gold potatoes, diced

1 (28-ounce) can crushed tomatoes

2 cups clam juice

1 (6.5-ounce) can chopped clams, juice drained and reserved

1 (10-ounce) can whole baby clams, juice drained and reserved

⅓ cup heavy (whipping) cream

Salt

Freshly ground black pepper

Freshly chopped flat-leaf parsley, for garnish

1. Turn on the electric pressure cooker and select the "Sauté" mode. Cook the bacon for 5 minutes, or until crisp. Retain about 1 tablespoon of fat in the pot. Transfer the bacon to a plate lined with paper towels and set aside.

2. Add the onion and garlic and cook for 2 minutes, or until the onion is soft. Turn off the "Sauté" mode.

3. Add the bay leaf, thyme, celery seed, red pepper flakes, carrot, celery, potatoes, crushed tomatoes, clam juice, and drained liquid from the canned clams, and stir to combine.

4. Secure the lid. Select the "Manual" mode, and set the cooking time for 7 minutes under High Pressure. When the cooking cycle is complete, quick release any remaining steam.

5. Select the "Sauté" mode again and bring the soup to a simmer. Then, stir in the chopped and whole canned clams and heavy cream and simmer until heated through. Turn the electric pressure cooker off.

6. Season with salt and pepper to taste. Garnish with parsley before serving.

TIP: If fresh littleneck or cherrystone clams are available, you can use them in place of the canned clams. Simply place the clams in a pot with water and steam them until they completely open. Remove the clams from their shells and chop them up. Strain the steaming liquid through a fine-mesh strainer to remove any grit and reserve the liquid in place of the clam juice called for in the recipe.

Per Serving: Calories: 383; Protein: 25g; Fat: 15g; Saturated Fat: 7g; Carbohydrates: 38g; Sugar: 11g; Sodium: 1,699mg; Fiber: 8g

PORTUGUESE-INSPIRED FISH AND SAUSAGE STEW

45 MINUTES OR LESS, DAIRY-FREE, GLUTEN-FREE

This stew is a great change of pace from the typical seafood stew and brings the flavors of earth and sea together. Seafood and sausage complement each other so well, and smoky, spicy linguica sausage provides a unique flavor. For a delicious accompaniment to the stew, toast a few thick slices of crusty bread and rub each piece with the cut side of a halved garlic clove while it's still warm. It's even better with a glass of *Vinho Verde*!

SERVES: 4

PREP TIME: 5 MINUTES

SAUTÉ TIME: 15 MINUTES

PRESSURIZATION TIME: 10 MINUTES

COOK TIME: 10 MINUTES ON "MANUAL" MODE UNDER HIGH PRESSURE

RELEASE: QUICK RELEASE

TOTAL TIME: 40 MINUTES

1 tablespoon olive oil

8 ounces linguica sausage, cut into ¼-inch pieces

1 onion, diced

1 red bell pepper, seeded and diced

3 garlic cloves, minced

1 teaspoon paprika

1 bay leaf

2 Yukon Gold potatoes, skin left on and cut into 1-inch pieces

1 (15-ounce) can no-salt-added diced tomatoes

½ cup dry white wine

3 cups Fish Stock (page 21) or store-bought unsalted fish stock or clam juice

1 pound littleneck clams and/or mussels, scrubbed

1½ pounds cod or other firm whitefish, cut into 2-inch pieces

Salt

Freshly ground black pepper

Freshly chopped flat-leaf parsley, for garnish

continued >

PORTUGUESE-INSPIRED FISH AND SAUSAGE STEW

continued

1. Turn on the electric pressure cooker and select the "Sauté" mode. Heat the olive oil and cook the linguica for 2 minutes, or until brown. Add the onion, bell pepper, and garlic and cook for 3 minutes, or until the vegetables are soft. Turn off the "Sauté" mode.

2. Add the paprika, bay leaf, potatoes, diced tomatoes with their juices, wine, and stock, and stir to combine.

3. Secure the lid. Select the "Manual" mode, and set the cooking time for 10 minutes under High Pressure. When the cooking cycle is complete, quick release any remaining steam.

4. Remove and discard the bay leaf.

5. Select the "Sauté" mode again and bring the stew to a simmer. Then, add the clams, cover with a glass lid (or regular lid, but do not lock it in place), and simmer for 5 minutes, or until they open.

6. Add the cod and simmer for 5 minutes, or until just cooked through. Turn the electric pressure cooker off.

7. Season the soup with salt and pepper to taste. Garnish with parsley before serving.

TIP: If you can't find linguica sausage, substitute any mildly spicy and smoked sausage such as Spanish chorizo or kielbasa.

Per Serving: Calories: 481; Protein: 51g; Fat: 15g; Saturated Fat: 4g; Carbohydrates: 32g; Sugar: 8g; Sodium: 1,028mg; Fiber: 5g

SALMON CHOWDER

45 MINUTES OR LESS, GLUTEN-FREE

Thick, creamy, and chock-full of delicious ingredients, this chowder is a taste of the Pacific Northwest in a bowl. I like to keep the fish in nice big chunks, but you can also flake them into smaller pieces after they've cooked. Use this recipe as a starting point for another fish chowder—smoked trout or haddock would be delicious too!

SERVES: 4

PREP TIME: 5 MINUTES

SAUTÉ TIME: 8 MINUTES

PRESSURIZATION TIME: 10 MINUTES

COOK TIME: 7 MINUTES ON "MANUAL" MODE UNDER HIGH PRESSURE

RELEASE: QUICK RELEASE

TOTAL TIME: 30 MINUTES

2 tablespoons unsalted butter

1 onion, diced

2 garlic cloves, minced

1 carrot, peeled and diced

2 celery stalks, diced

2 red potatoes, diced

1 cup fresh or frozen corn kernels

½ teaspoon dried thyme

½ teaspoon dill weed

3 cups Fish Stock (page 21) or Chicken Broth (page 16) or store-bought unsalted fish stock or chicken broth

2 tablespoons cornstarch

2 cups half-and-half

½ cup frozen peas

1-pound salmon fillet, skinned and cut into 1-inch pieces

1 teaspoon fresh lemon juice

Salt

Freshly ground black pepper

Freshly chopped dill, for garnish

continued >

SALMON CHOWDER

continued

1. Turn on the electric pressure cooker and select the "Sauté" mode. Melt the butter and cook the onion and garlic for 2 minutes, or until the onion is soft. Turn off the "Sauté" mode.

2. Add the carrot, celery, potatoes, corn, thyme, dill weed, and stock, and stir to combine.

3. Secure the lid. Select the "Manual" mode, and set the cooking time for 7 minutes under High Pressure. When the cooking cycle is complete, quick release any remaining steam.

4. In a separate bowl, whisk together the cornstarch and half-and-half. Select the "Sauté" mode again and bring the soup to a simmer. Then, add the cornstarch mixture and stir for 1 minute, or until the soup has thickened.

5. Add the frozen peas and salmon to the soup and simmer for 5 minutes, or until the fish is just cooked through. Turn the electric pressure cooker off.

6. Add the lemon juice and season with salt and pepper to taste. Garnish with dill before serving.

TIP: If fresh salmon is not available, a good-quality canned salmon can be used in a pinch. It's not as good as fresh, but it works surprisingly well for a last-minute option.

Per Serving: Calories: 527; Protein: 36g; Fat: 24g; Saturated Fat: 13g; Carbohydrates: 43g; Sugar: 13g; Sodium: 284mg; Fiber: 5.5g

BRAZILIAN-INSPIRED FISH STEW (MOQUECA)

45 MINUTES OR LESS, DAIRY-FREE, GLUTEN-FREE

Moqueca is a popular Brazilian fish stew with strong African roots from the Bahia state. Often slow-simmered in clay pots, this stew comes together quickly in the electric pressure cooker and is a delicious new way to enjoy fish. Dendê oil (also known as red palm oil) is traditionally used, which adds to the authenticity of the dish, but coconut oil and vegetable oil are great substitutes. Finish this dish with a squeeze of fresh lime juice and cilantro and serve it over steamed rice for a nice bit of tropical flair.

SERVES: 4

PREP TIME: 5 MINUTES

SAUTÉ TIME: 12 MINUTES

PRESSURIZATION TIME:
10 MINUTES

COOK TIME: 10 MINUTES ON
"MANUAL" MODE UNDER HIGH
PRESSURE

RELEASE: QUICK RELEASE

TOTAL TIME: 37 MINUTES

1 tablespoon coconut or vegetable oil

1 onion, diced

4 garlic cloves, minced

1 green bell pepper, seeded and diced

1 carrot, diced

1 tablespoon paprika

1 teaspoon ground cumin

¼ teaspoon cayenne pepper

1 (15-ounce) can crushed tomatoes

1 (14-ounce) can coconut milk

1 cup Fish Stock (page 21) or Vegetable Broth (page 14) or store-bought unsalted fish stock or vegetable broth

1½ pounds firm whitefish (like sea bass or halibut), cut into 2-inch pieces

1 tablespoon fresh lime juice

Salt

Freshly ground black pepper

Freshly chopped cilantro, for garnish

continued >

BRAZILIAN-INSPIRED FISH STEW (MOQUECA)

continued

1. Turn on the electric pressure cooker and select the "Sauté" mode. Heat the coconut oil and cook the onion and garlic for 2 minutes, or until the onion is soft. Turn off the "Sauté" mode.

2. Add the bell pepper, carrot, paprika, cumin, cayenne pepper, tomatoes, coconut milk, and stock, and stir to combine.

3. Secure the lid. Select the "Manual" mode, and set the cooking time for 10 minutes under High Pressure. When the cooking cycle is complete, quick release any remaining steam.

4. Select the "Sauté" mode again and bring the stew to a simmer. Let the stew simmer for 5 minutes, or until it thickens. Add the whitefish to the stew and simmer for 5 minutes or until just cooked through. Turn the electric pressure cooker off.

5. Add the lime juice and season with salt and pepper to taste. Garnish with cilantro before serving.

TIP: For this recipe, as well as others that call for firm whitefish, you can choose one depending on your budget and the quality of what is available, as long as the fish is mildly flavored and can hold up to the simmering process. Sea bass, cod, pollock, haddock, monkfish, and grouper are all good options.

Per Serving: Calories: 466; Protein: 37g; Fat: 28g; Saturated Fat: 22g; Carbohydrates: 18g; Sugar: 6.5g; Sodium: 363mg; Fiber: 5.5g

COD AND POTATO STEW

45 MINUTES OR LESS, GLUTEN-FREE

Stew doesn't have to take hours to prepare. In fact, this one-pot meal is an ideal combination of low effort and high return. There aren't a ton of ingredients here, but each of them makes a big impact and provides an abundance of flavor. Use whatever fish you can find at your fish market, as long as it is not too oily and has a firm texture that holds up to the stew without falling apart.

SERVES: 4

PREP TIME: 5 MINUTES

SAUTÉ TIME: 9 MINUTES

PRESSURIZATION TIME: 6 MINUTES

COOK TIME: 10 MINUTES ON "MANUAL" MODE UNDER HIGH PRESSURE

RELEASE: QUICK RELEASE

TOTAL TIME: 30 MINUTES

2 tablespoons olive oil

2 shallots, diced

1 fennel bulb, fronds removed and diced

2 garlic cloves, minced

8 ounces baby Yukon Gold or red potatoes, halved

½ cup dry white wine

2 cups Fish Stock (page 21) or Chicken Broth (page 16) or store-bought unsalted fish stock or chicken broth

1½ pounds cod, cut into 2-inch pieces

¼ cup crème fraîche

2 tablespoons freshly chopped dill

Salt

Freshly ground black pepper

continued >

COD AND POTATO STEW

continued

1. Turn on the electric pressure cooker and select the "Sauté" mode. Heat the olive oil and cook the shallots, fennel, and garlic for 4 minutes, or until the vegetables are soft. Turn off the "Sauté" mode.

2. Add the potatoes, wine, and stock, and stir to combine.

3. Secure the lid. Select the "Manual" mode, and set the cooking time for 10 minutes under High Pressure. When the cooking cycle is complete, quick release any remaining steam.

4. Select the "Sauté" mode again and bring the stew to a simmer. Then, add the cod to the stew and simmer for 5 minutes, or until just cooked through. Turn the electric pressure cooker off.

5. Stir in the crème fraîche and dill. Season with salt and pepper to taste.

TIP: Crème fraîche gives the stew a nice tang and creaminess. If you can't find it, you can substitute sour cream or Greek yogurt, though they're not nearly as rich and creamy and are a bit tangier than crème fraîche.

Per Serving: Calories: 357; Protein: 35g; Fat: 13g; Saturated Fat: 4.5g; Carbohydrates: 21g; Sugar: 6.5g; Sodium: 268mg; Fiber: 4.5g

MARYLAND-STYLE CRAB BISQUE

Growing up on the East Coast gives you every excuse to eat as much fresh seafood as you can. In the summer months, our family often made road trips to Maryland to get our fill of their prized steamed blue crabs. If you can't make your way to the crab shacks, the next best thing you can do is enjoy the flavors in the form of this bisque. You won't be disappointed!

SERVES: 4

PREP TIME: 5 MINUTES

SAUTÉ TIME: 5 MINUTES

PRESSURIZATION TIME: 10 MINUTES

COOK TIME: 10 MINUTES ON "MANUAL" MODE UNDER HIGH PRESSURE

RELEASE: QUICK RELEASE

TOTAL TIME: 30 MINUTES

2 tablespoons unsalted butter

1 onion, diced

2 garlic cloves, minced

1 carrot, diced

1 celery stalk, diced

3 tablespoons all-purpose flour

1½ teaspoons Old Bay seasoning

1 tablespoon tomato paste

¼ cup dry sherry or white wine

4 cups Shellfish Stock (page 20) or Vegetable Broth (page 14) or store-bought unsalted shellfish stock or vegetable broth

8 ounces lump crabmeat

½ cup heavy (whipping) cream

Salt

Freshly ground black pepper

Freshly chopped flat-leaf parsley, for garnish

continued >

MARYLAND-STYLE CRAB BISQUE

continued

1. Turn on the electric pressure cooker and select the "Sauté" mode. Melt the butter and cook the onion, garlic, carrot, and celery for 4 minutes, or until the vegetables are soft. Add the flour and cook for 1 minute, or until the vegetables are well coated. Turn off the "Sauté" mode.

2. Add the Old Bay seasoning, tomato paste, sherry, and stock, and stir to combine.

3. Secure the lid. Select the "Manual" mode, and set the cooking time for 10 minutes under High Pressure. When the cooking cycle is complete, quick release any remaining steam.

4. Using an immersion blender, traditional blender, or food processor, blend the soup until smooth.

5. Select the "Sauté" mode again and bring the soup to a simmer. Then, stir in the crabmeat and heavy cream and simmer until heated through. Turn the electric pressure cooker off.

6. Season with salt and pepper to taste. Garnish with parsley before serving.

TIP: This bisque will work with any kind of fresh crabmeat, such as Maryland blue crab, Dungeness crab, or even Alaskan king crab. Don't use canned crabmeat, though, as the taste and texture are not quite right for this recipe.

Per Serving: Calories: 263; Protein: 12g; Fat: 17g; Saturated Fat: 11g; Carbohydrates: 14g; Sugar: 4.5g; Sodium: 318mg; Fiber: 2g

SPICY TOMATO AND CRAB SOUP

When it comes to shellfish—especially crab—I have all the patience in the world. I can sit for hours with a mallet, carefully picking the sweet, briny crabmeat from the shells. With the easy accessibility of fresh lump crabmeat at most seafood counters or seafood markets, this spicy tomato and crab soup couldn't be easier or more convenient. While this isn't an everyday soup, when you do make it, I'm sure you'll love every bite.

SERVES: 4

PREP TIME: 5 MINUTES

SAUTÉ TIME: 2 MINUTES

PRESSURIZATION TIME: 10 MINUTES

COOK TIME: 10 MINUTES ON "MANUAL" MODE UNDER HIGH PRESSURE

RELEASE: QUICK RELEASE

TOTAL TIME: 27 MINUTES

2 tablespoons olive oil

1 onion, diced

3 garlic cloves, minced

1½ pounds plum tomatoes, seeded and coarsely chopped

1 red bell pepper, seeded and coarsely chopped

1 jalapeño pepper, seeded and coarsely chopped

¼ teaspoon cayenne pepper

½ teaspoon Old Bay seasoning

1 teaspoon Worcestershire sauce

2 tablespoons tomato paste

3 cups Shellfish Stock (page 20) or Vegetable Broth (page 14) or store-bought unsalted shellfish stock or vegetable broth

8 ounces lump crabmeat

Salt

Freshly ground black pepper

Freshly chopped flat-leaf parsley, for garnish

continued >

SPICY TOMATO AND CRAB SOUP

continued

1. Turn on the electric pressure cooker and select the "Sauté" mode. Heat the olive oil and cook the onion and garlic for 2 minutes, or until the onion is soft. Turn off the "Sauté" mode.

2. Add the tomatoes, bell pepper, jalapeño pepper, cayenne pepper, Old Bay seasoning, Worcestershire sauce, tomato paste, and stock, and stir to combine.

3. Secure the lid. Select the "Manual" mode, and set the cooking time for 10 minutes under High Pressure. When the cooking cycle is complete, quick release any remaining steam.

4. Using an immersion blender, traditional blender, or food processor, blend the soup until smooth.

5. Select the "Sauté" mode again and bring the soup to a simmer. Then, stir in the crabmeat and simmer until heated through. Turn the electric pressure cooker off.

6. Season with salt and pepper to taste. Garnish with parsley before serving.

TIP: When using lump crabmeat, try to avoid stirring the soup too much. You don't want to break up the lumps since they have such a nice texture when they're kept intact.

Per Serving: Calories: 172; Protein: 12g; Fat: 8g; Saturated Fat: 1g; Carbohydrates: 16g; Sugar: 9g; Sodium: 324mg; Fiber: 4g

LOBSTER AND CORN CHOWDER

45 MINUTES OR LESS, GLUTEN-FREE

Serve this chowder as the entrée topped with some oyster crackers and a fresh green salad on the side, or as part of a hefty surf-and-turf feast. This is an admittedly decadent soup, but don't be tempted to replace the heavy cream with milk because every single bite of this lobster and corn goodness is worth it.

SERVES: 4

PREP TIME: 5 MINUTES

SAUTÉ TIME: 9 MINUTES

PRESSURIZATION TIME:
10 MINUTES

COOK TIME: 7 MINUTES ON "MANUAL" MODE UNDER HIGH PRESSURE

RELEASE: QUICK RELEASE

TOTAL TIME: 31 MINUTES

4 bacon slices, diced

2 leeks (white and light green parts only), thinly sliced

2 celery stalks, diced

2 Yukon Gold or red potatoes, skin left on and diced

3 cups fresh or frozen corn kernels

4 cups lobster stock

1 tablespoon cornstarch

1 cup heavy (whipping) cream

2 cups cooked lobster meat, cut into bite-size pieces

Salt

Freshly ground black pepper

2 tablespoons freshly chopped chives

continued >

LOBSTER AND CORN CHOWDER

continued

1. Turn on the electric pressure cooker and select the "Sauté" mode. Cook the bacon for 5 minutes, or until crisp. Retain about 1 tablespoon of fat in the pot. Transfer the bacon to a plate lined with paper towels and set aside.

2. Add the leeks and celery and cook for 3 minutes, or until the vegetables start to become soft. Turn off the "Sauté" mode.

3. Add the potatoes, corn, stock, and cooked bacon, and stir to combine.

4. Secure the lid. Select the "Manual" mode, and set the cooking time for 7 minutes under High Pressure. When the cooking cycle is complete, quick release any remaining steam.

5. In a separate bowl, whisk together the cornstarch and heavy cream. Select the "Sauté" mode again and bring the soup to a simmer. Then, add the cornstarch mixture and stir for 1 minute, or until the soup has thickened. Stir in the lobster meat and simmer until heated through. Turn the electric pressure cooker off.

6. Season with salt and pepper to taste. Garnish with chives before serving.

TIP: If you can get fresh corn on the cob, shuck the corn and reserve the kernels for use, then add the cobs to the pot when making the stock for additional sweet corn flavor.

Per Serving: Calories: 565; Protein: 29g; Fat: 30g; Saturated Fat: 16g; Carbohydrates: 50g; Sugar: 13g; Sodium: 551mg; Fiber: 5.5g

Measurement Conversions

VOLUME EQUIVALENTS (LIQUID)

US STANDARD	US STANDARD (OUNCES)	METRIC (APPROXIMATE)
2 tablespoons	1 fl. oz.	30 mL
¼ cup	2 fl. oz.	60 mL
½ cup	4 fl. oz.	120 mL
1 cup	8 fl. oz.	240 mL
1½ cups	12 fl. oz.	355 mL
2 cups or 1 pint	16 fl. oz.	475 mL
4 cups or 1 quart	32 fl. oz.	1 L
1 gallon	128 fl. oz.	4 L

OVEN TEMPERATURES

FAHRENHEIT	CELSIUS (APPROXIMATE)
250°F	120°C
300°F	150°C
325°F	165°C
350°F	180°C
375°F	190°C
400°F	200°C
425°F	220°C
450°F	230°C

VOLUME EQUIVALENTS (DRY)

US STANDARD	METRIC (APPROXIMATE)
⅛ teaspoon	0.5 mL
¼ teaspoon	1 mL
½ teaspoon	2 mL
¾ teaspoon	4 mL
1 teaspoon	5 mL
1 tablespoon	15 mL
¼ cup	59 mL
⅓ cup	79 mL
½ cup	118 mL
⅔ cup	156 mL
¾ cup	177 mL
1 cup	235 mL
2 cups or 1 pint	475 mL
3 cups	700 mL
4 cups or 1 quart	1 L

WEIGHT EQUIVALENTS

US STANDARD	METRIC (APPROXIMATE)
½ ounce	15 g
1 ounce	30 g
2 ounces	60 g
4 ounces	115 g
8 ounces	225 g
12 ounces	340 g
16 ounces or 1 pound	455 g

Index

Acknowledgments

Writing this book would not have been possible without the efforts of many people. Thanks to the publishing team at Callisto Media and my editor, Gurvinder, for their support, partnership, and guidance in shaping the vision of this book and making it a reality.

Thank you to my family and friends, who provided so much support in the creation of this project, always ready to be my taste testers and provide invaluable suggestions and constructive feedback. My parents, David and Linda, for showing me the value of sharing a home-cooked meal with family. My siblings, Carol and Kelly, who have always fed my culinary enthusiasm and helped shape how I cook today. My husband, James, whose encouragement and support have inspired me to pursue this endeavor, and who is always ready to taste every soup I make for months again and again without complaints and kindly cleans up after all the messes I make in the kitchen.

About the Author

Karen Lee Young is the founder of *The Tasty Bite*, a food blog featuring recipes that make cooking from scratch as simple as possible for both novice and experienced home cooks. Her work has been featured in the *Huffington Post*, *Country Living*, Buzzfeed, *Greatist*, and many other media outlets. Originally from New York City, she now lives in Colorado with her husband and daughter. When Karen is not in the kitchen, you'll find her enjoying the outdoors, exploring different restaurants, and traveling near and far.